THE ELEMENTS OF

Janis Huntley has been a practising a
and has given hundreds of private rea
for Surrey evening class institutions a

The *Elements Of* is a series designed to present high quality introductions to a broad range of essential subjects.

The books are commissioned specifically from experts in their fields. They provide readable and often unique views of the various topics covered, and are therefore of interest both to those who have some knowledge of the subject, as well as those who are approaching it for the first time.

Many of these concise yet comprehensive books have practical suggestions and exercises which allow personal experiences as well as theoretical understanding, and offer a valuable source of information on many important themes.

In the same series

Aborigine Tradition
Alchemy
The Arthurian Tradition
The Bahá'i Faith
Buddhism
Celtic Christianity
The Celtic Tradition
The Chakras
Christian Symbolism
Creation Myth
Dreamwork
The Druid Tradition
Earth Mysteries
Feng Shui
Gnosticism
The Goddess
The Grail Tradition
The Greek Tradition
Herbalism
Human Potential
Islam
Meditation
Mysticism
Native American Traditions
Natural Magic
Pendulum Dowsing
Prophecy
Psychosynthesis
The Qabalah
Shamanism
Sufism
Tai Chi
Taoism
Visualisation
Zen

THE ELEMENTS OF

ASTROLOGY

Janis Huntley

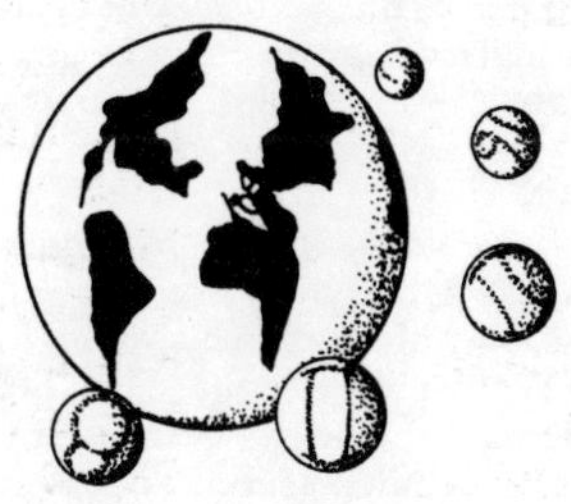

ELEMENT
Shaftesbury, Dorset • Rockport, Massachusetts
Brisbane, Queensland

Published in Great Britain in 1990 by
Element Books Limited
Longmead, Shaftesbury, Dorset

Published in the USA by
Element Inc.
42 Broadway, Rockport, MA 01966

First published in Australia by
Element Boks Ltd for
Jacaranda Wiley Ltd
33 Park Road, Milton, Brisbane 4064

Reprinted September 1990
Reprinted 1993
Reprinted 1994

Designed by Jenny Liddle
Cover design by Max Fairbrother
Cover illustration by Martin Rieser
Typeset by Selectmove Ltd, London
Printed and bound in Great Britain by
Biddles Limited, Guildford & King's Lynn

British Library Cataloguing in Publication Data
Huntley, Janis
The elements of astrology
1. Astrology
I. Title
133.5

Library of Congress Cataloging in Publication
data available

ISBN 1–85230–135–X

CONTENTS

FOREWORD

I have always been baffled by the aura of complexity and mystery which seems to surround the issue of learning astrology. 'I couldn't possibly absorb all that!' or 'I'd love to be able to work out a birth chart but it looks far too involved for me' – these are typical of the comments I have heard repeatedly throughout the many years of my teaching experience in astrology.

It's not surprising, however, when you glance at some of the textbooks available on the subject – all excellent books in their own right – to find that few of them cater for the average person who would like to learn about astrology for their own interest, rather than to study over a period of several years, take a diploma, and become a professional astrologer.

It is in this respect that my book differs. For those of you who would like to learn astrology without too much effort or mathematical genius, this book in indispensable. Using my own simple system of guidance, most students can erect a birth chart and understand the basic principles of interpretation after only ten lessons. Much of the laborious mathematical calculation has been eliminated – but for those who baulk at the minimal amount of mathematics required, there are many good computer chart calculation services offered nowadays. The only details required are date, place and time of birth.

Although the course is simplified, high standards of accuracy are adhered to. The main criterion in erecting a birth chart is the time of birth, but the *precise* moment of birth is not easily defined. Is it our first breath, or is it the actual moment we emerge from the womb? There is always some discrepancy – a factor which tends to defeat the objective of the fanatical astrologer who insists upon working out the birth chart from the exact minute and second of birth! Interpretation is the most important consideration in astrology, and good interpretative readings do not depend upon precise mathematical calculations. It does not matter how long you take to complete this Course, but even if you spend a whole month on each lesson you will have finished in ten months, which is less than half the time it takes to complete a typical diploma course! Good luck in your endeavours.

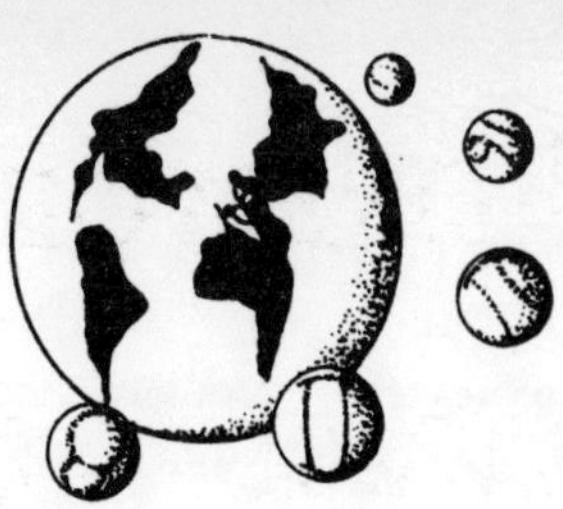

1 · Introduction to Signs and Planets

In this first lesson I am going to introduce you to the basic tools of interpretative astrology, namely the twelve signs of the zodiac and the ten known planets of our solar system. (For any astronomers reading this book, I will mention now that for convenience sake astrologers regard the Sun and Moon as planets, their use in birth chart interpretation being in accordance with the remaining eight planets.)

In order for you to progress swiftly to erecting an individual's birth chart (explained in Lesson 3) it is vital that you learn thoroughly the natural sequence of the signs and planets, their astrological symbols, and a few important keywords of interpretation. When you feel you have achieved this objective, answer the questions at the end of the lesson without referring to the text, then check your responses with the answers at the back of the book. Ideally, as with all the lessons, you should aim for seven or more correct replies. Having reached this target you are ready to progress onto the next lesson. I would strongly recommend anybody scoring lower than five marks to read the lesson through again and reattempt the test when they feel more competent to move on. It is important not to become discouraged as everybody learns at a different pace and the slow learner is often more painstakingly careful.

SIGNS OF THE ZODIAC

ARIES: The Ram (21 March to 19 April) Symbol: ♈

Keyword characteristics
Dominant, energetic, extroverted, impulsive, impatient, self-seeking, adventurous, argumentative, ardent, outspoken, hot-tempered.

Appearance: Irregular bold features. Angular face. Medium height. Often red or sandy-coloured hair with receding hairline in men.

TAURUS: The Bull (20 April to 20 May) Symbol: ♉

Keyword characteristics
Steady, reliable, materialistic, stubborn, musical, plodding, practical, green-fingered, sturdy, domesticated, loyal.

Appearance: Large, solid build. Square jaw. Thick curly hair, often dark. Short to medium height.

GEMINI: The Twins (21 May to 21 June) Symbol: ♊

Keyword characteristics
Lively, versatile, highly strung, moody, communicative, Jack of all trades, unemotional, unsympathetic, gesticulative, independent.

Appearance: Medium height to tall, with slim build. Twinkling eyes. Long arms or legs. Expressive hands. Attractive features.

CANCER: The Crab (22 June to 22 July) Symbol: ♋

Keyword characteristics
Sensitive, protective, nurturing, clinging, sentimental, quiet, home-loving, security-orientated, sarcastic, reticent, kind.

Appearance: Face either pale and round or sanguine and sharp. Blonde or black hair, usually sparse. Build plump and short.

LEO: The Lion (23 July to 22 August) Symbol: ♌

Keyword characteristics
Proud, egocentric, fun-loving, loud, bombastic, generous, lazy, determined, showy, theatrical, likeable, unrelenting, bossy.

Appearance: Thick wavy, blonde or red hair drawn back from the face. Sunny expression. Females usually well-adorned. Height medium to tall, often corpulent.

VIRGO: The Virgin (23 August to 22 September) Symbol: ♍

Keyword characteristics
Analytical, conscientious, discerning, critical, cool, fussy, intelligent, communicative, organising, retiring, diligent, restless, modest.

Appearance: Medium to tall build. Men usually slim in youth. Females tend to be plump. Staring or studious expression. Often lively or talkative exterior.

LIBRA: The Scales (23 September to 22 October) Symbol: ♎

Keyword characteristics
Well balanced, indecisive, fair, serene, self-absorbed, charming, polite, refined, lacking depth, sociable, impractical.

Appearance: Medium to tall build. Prone to plumpness in later years. Attractive. Men often effeminate. Round or oval face. Sleek hair.

SCORPIO: The Scorpion (23 October to 21 November) Symbol: ♏

Keyword characteristics
Secretive, emotional, intense, highly-sexed, possessive, jealous, spiritual, penetrating, sharp, observant, determined, unshakeable, generous or stringent to a fault.

Appearance: Square face. Deepset, or large round eyes which exude magnetism. Stocky build. Females curvaceous. Thick hair. Wide, straight mouth.

SAGITTARIUS: The Archer (22 November to 21 December) Symbol: ♐

Keyword characteristics
Frank, blunt, outspoken, honest, chatty, knowledgeable, freedom-seeking, restless, unreliable, changeable, optimistic, good-humoured, quick-tempered.

Appearance: Tall and slim, becoming larger with increasing years. Long, oval face. Lustrous, wavy, red or dark hair. Expressive eyes.

CAPRICORN: The Goat (22 December to 19 January) Symbol: ♑

Keyword characteristics
Cautious, shy, insecure, prudent, reliable, practical, down-to-earth, ambitious, status-seeking, reserved, sensuous, hard-working.

Appearance: Small, slim or bony frame. Thin fine hair, usually dark. Retain youthful appearance into old age. Serious expression.

AQUARIUS: The Water Carrier (20 January to 18 February) Symbol: ♒

Keyword characteristics
Outgoing, friendly, detached, humanitarian, impersonal, self-opinionated, eccentric, clever, ingenious, talented, unemotional.

Appearance: Attractive, even features. Square-set jaw, or pronounced chin. Usually dark-haired. Tall and slim in youth.

PISCES: The Fishes (19 February to 20 March) Symbol: ♓

Keyword characteristics
Dreamy, emotional, sensitive, shy, confused, escapist, introverted, artistic, vague, immoral, adaptable, muddle-headed, moody.

Appearance: Build, anything from extremely tall to extremely short. Large, protuberant or attractive eyes. Tendency to plumpness. Something untidy or chaotic about outer demeanour.

It is important to note that the dates given for the change of signs are only approximate, and can vary by as much as two whole days in any given year. In Lesson 3 you will learn how to read an astrological ephemeris, which gives exact times and dates when the Sun and other planets change sign.

Now on to the planets, which are undoubtedly the most important tools of astrological interpretation. Each of the ten planets commonly used in astrology possesses its own unique characteristics, and is designated to rule one particular sign of the zodiac. However, as you may already have deduced, there are only ten planets to go round the twelve signs. Therefore the two planets Venus and Mercury hold the enviable task of ruling two signs of the zodiac each.

Sun	☉	Rules Leo
Moon	☽	Rules Cancer
Mercury	☿	Rules Gemini and Virgo
Venus	♀	Rules Taurus and Libra
Mars	♂	Rules Aries
Jupiter	♃	Rules Sagittarius
Saturn	♄	Rules Capricorn
Uranus	♅	Rules Aquarius
Neptune	♆	Rules Pisces
Pluto	♇	Rules Scorpio (see footnote opposite*)

Note: Prior to the last three planets (Uranus, Neptune and Pluto) being discovered, the sign of Aquarius was ruled by Saturn, Pisces was ruled by Jupiter, and Scorpio was ruled by Mars.

Each of the above planets takes a certain length of time to circle around the earth and encompass the twelve signs of the zodiac. The Moon, which is the fastest-moving planet, takes only twenty-eight days to orbit the earth and spends approximately two and a half days in one sign of the zodiac, whereas Pluto the outermost planet can spend up to thirty years in one sign alone.

It is for this reason that the planets are divided into three distinct divisions:

Sun Moon Mercury Venus Mars	These first five planets move relatively swiftly and are therefore regarded as *PERSONAL* planets.
Jupiter Saturn	These move more slowly and are regarded as the two *MIDDLE* planets.
Uranus Neptune Pluto	Extremely slow-moving, these are the three outer planets, which tend to be more generational in their effect.

Each planet represents a certain method of expressing ourselves:

The **Sun** is our ego, our individuality, the essential core of our whole character. It relates to how we view ourselves on an inner level.

For example: Do you regard yourself as confident, impulsive and brash as the Sun in Aries would, or do you see yourself as being cautious, shy, lacking in confidence, as is more typical of the Sun in Capricorn?

The **Moon** represents our emotions, feelings, responses and habits, and is very important in the birth charts of children.

For example: Do you respond to a stressful situation with sensitivity, tears and shyness, as would a person with Moon in Pisces, or would you analyse the situation and talk matters over in the typical manner of somebody who has the Moon in Virgo or Gemini?

Mercury rules the manner in which we communicate, through speech, thought, learning or writing. It is strongly associated with the mind.

* This is the original, precise symbol for the planet Pluto. Many astrologers now prefer to use the updated symbol, written thus: ⯓ which is regarded as being more spiritual. To avoid confusion with the similar symbol for the planet Neptune I will use the version ♇ throughout this book.

For example: Do you talk in a forthright, open manner, as the person with Mercury in Sagittarius does, or are you more of a 'deep thinker' than a conversationalist like somebody with Mercury in Scorpio?

Venus indicates how we love, what we appreciate and value in life, our strivings for perfection and harmony.

For example: Do you love protectively, nurturingly, caringly, and value your home, as would someone with Venus in Cancer, or do you tend to love detachedly, at a distance, perhaps valuing companionship and communication more than romance, like the person with Venus in Aquarius?

Mars rules the amount of energy and drive we possess, our sexuality, aggressive tendencies, and self-seeking characteristics.

For example: Is much of your energy directed towards materialism, or nature conservation as would be typical of the person with Mars in Taurus, or is your energy diverse, changeable, emotionally unstable, or confused, as could occur with Mars in Pisces?

Jupiter represents the manner in which we expand ourselves. It is also indicative of our religious and philosophical beliefs. This planet can make us feel on top of the world. For example: Do you endeavour to expand your charm, fairness and balance like someone with Jupiter in Libra, or are you extremely concerned with minor details – making mountains out of molehills, and enjoying analytical work, such as the person with Jupiter in Virgo?

Saturn is the planet of learning. It can therefore restrict, limit and burden our lives with serious intent. This planet can often make us depressed or down in the dumps.

For example: Do you feel restricted or frustrated in your innate desire to be a gregarious extrovert,or a distinguished celebrity, as would a person with Saturn in Leo, or do you feel at ease in ponderous, grave situations, with ample time to work matters out thoroughly, like somebody with Saturn in Capricorn?

Uranus rules everything that is unusual, or happens suddenly in our lives. It can disrupt, be extremely unconventional and rebellious, yet also exciting.

For example: Are you a live-wire who is stimulated by change, variety, knowledge and learning, which is indicative of Uranus placed in Gemini, or do you feel threatened by life's ups and downs, yet often find that you are forced by circumstances to change your environment, jobs, attitudes, etc., as could happen with Uranus placed in Taurus?

Neptune is the planet of mystery. It rules escapism confusion, spirituality. It is nebulous and difficult to understand, being indicative of the subconscious on a very deep level. It can cast us down to evil depths, or elevate us into the highest elements of love and creativity.

For example: Do you sometimes feel as if you are not truly of this world – that there is something or somebody out there ruling your life, directing you into good or evil, as might be the experience of a person with Neptune in Pisces, or are you a highly practical person, who for no logical reason, occasionally becomes confused and irrational about the fundamental, materialistic side of life, as could happen with Neptune placed in the sign of Capricorn.

Pluto is a tiny, but powerful planet. It tends to rule behind the scenes and invariably comes out on top. It is significant of eruptions, transformations, birth, death and rebirth.

For example: Were you born in the 1940s or 1950s during the generation of people born with Pluto situated in the sign of Leo (indicating that your personal ego and individuality would be dogged throughout your life by major upheavals and the need for transformation)? Or, were you born in the 1960s when the mighty power of Pluto moving through the mundane, critical sign of Virgo, created a generation of highly strung, restless individuals continually striving to cope with the stress caused by the intensity of eruptive Pluto in such a practical, reserved sign.

This brief introduction to the signs and planets (we shall be studying them in more depth later on in this book) should enable you to attempt the following test, endeavouring to use symbols, wherever appropriate.

1 Which sign follows on from Aries in the zodiac?
2. Write the symbol for the sign Capricorn.
3. Name at least one of the qualities or principles embodied in the planet Mars.
4. Name the three outer planets.
5. Name the five personal planets.
6. Describe in as many words as you can some of the characteristics of the sign Leo.
7. Name the planetary ruler for the signs Gemini and Virgo.
8. Give at least one word to describe the planet Uranus.
9. Expansion is one of the keywords for which planet?
10. Freedom-loving, blunt, outspoken and honest. Which sign of the zodiac am I describing?

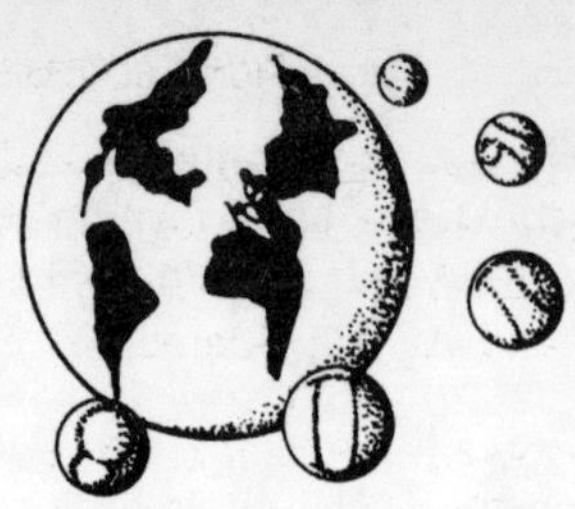

2 · SIGN GROUPINGS AND INTERPRETATIONS

The signs of the zodiac can be divided into three major interpretive groups, all of which are extremely important in the summarising of an individual's character. This lesson will teach you how to classify a person into the broad categories of extrovert or introvert, dependable or changeable, etc.

ACTIVE AND PASSIVE

The twelve signs are divided into two groups of six, which are labelled Active/Passive (or Masculine/Feminine, or Positive/Negative). Having already learnt the sequence of the signs of the zodiac it is easy to apportion each sign to its appropriate heading. Starting with the sign of Aries, which is *active*, every alternate and odd-numbered sign, ending with the eleventh sign of Aquarius, is also *active*. Commencing with the second sign of Taurus, which is *passive*, each alternate and even-numbered sign, ending with the twelfth sign of Pisces, is also *passive*.

Active Signs		*Passive Signs*	
Aries	Libra	Taurus	Scorpio
Gemini	Sagittarius	Cancer	Capricorn
Leo	Aquarius	Virgo	Pisces

Active signs tend to react forcefully, energetically, positively, unthinkingly. Typically, they are the head first, feet later, individuals who are relatively confident of their position in life. They lack introspectiveness, and are considered to be the extroverts of the zodiac.

Passive signs are more contemplative. They can be retiring, unforthcoming and reticent. They are rarely impulsive, or showy, and often prefer to work quietly behind the scenes, but because they think before they act, they often come up trumps, eventually succeeding where the Active person can fail. They are the introverts of the zodiac. The majority of people however are a blend of Active and Passive, with one factor slightly dominant, and it is very rare to find an individual with all ten planets situated in one specific group.

THE FOUR ELEMENTS

In this extremely important division of the zodiac, four groups of three signs are allocated a certain element, Fire, Earth, Air or Water:

FIRE	*EARTH*	*AIR*	*WATER*
Aries	Taurus	Gemini	Cancer
Leo	Virgo	Libra	Scorpio
Sagittarius	Capricorn	Aquarius	Pisces

You will note from the above that all the Fire and Air signs are Active and all the Earth and Water are Passive. Each of the four elements possesses favourable, positive characteristics and detrimental negative characteristics, as listed below. (Do not confuse the terms positive and negative used in this instance, with the division of active and passive above.)

FIRE

These signs can be ardent, enthusiastic, energetic, warm, outgoing, forthright, honest, uncomplicated, optimistic, adventurous, magnetic,

or

Aggressive, domineering, blunt, offensive, impatient, egotistical, chauvinistic, thoughtless, itinerant, hot-tempered.

EARTH

This element can produce people who are steady, reliable, practical, down-to earth, businesslike, loyal, sensible, upright, hardworking, patient, analytical, precise,
or
dull, materialistic, ruthless, critical, lascivious, mean, slovenly, over-serious, stubborn, self-righteous, depressive.

AIR

People born with many planets in this element are usually communicative, lively, intellectual, resourceful, inventive, calm, logical, charming, sociable, talented,
or
self-opiniated, detached, cold, haughty, impractical, eccentric, highly strung, lacking in direction, unfeeling.

WATER

Individuals with this element strong in their chart can be sensitive, kind, protective, artistic, caring, sacrificial, sympathetic, supportive, intuitive, easy-going, spiritual,
or
grasping, over-emotional, controlling, addictive, lacking in standards or morals, untidy, dreamy, destructive, revengeful.

Ideally, in order to be a well-adjusted individual in society we should all possess an even balance of the above elements. More often than not, however, one or two elements predominate within our birth chart, causing imbalance, problems, and challenges throughout the life.

QUADRUPLICITIES

The signs can be further divided into the following three groups of four:

Cardinal		*Fixed*		*Mutable*	
Aries	Fire	Taurus	Earth	Gemini	Air
Cancer	Water	Leo	Fire	Virgo	Earth
Libra	Air	Scorpio	Water	Sagittarius	Fire
Capricorn	Earth	Aquarius	Air	Pisces	Water

You will notice that all three groups are formed by taking one sign from each of the four elements. Contrary and diverse as this may seem, all of the four signs in each group possess a certain similarity of character described below:

CARDINAL

Cardinal signs seek out what they want in life, pushing themselves to the forefront of activity, making sure that their voices are somehow heard in the crowd. They are regarded as the self-starters, the initiators of the zodiac and can often appear self-centred. Each sign within this group, however, tends to push itself in a different manner:

Aries (cardinal fire) pushes with brashness and physical force. Lacking in finesse, a strongly Aries person will think nothing of bullying their way to the front of the queue or leading a group of people with brave, reckless abandon. Ariens will always make themselves conspicuous in the most direct manner possible but they can be daring, exciting people with a love of adventure.

Cancer (cardinal water) pushes with slow, sideways movements. They are far too easily hurt to consider aiming directly for their objectives, so they move in a seemingly indifferent, round-about manner, only pouncing when they are sure of acceptance. They will also endeavour to achieve their own ends by appealing to the emotions of others – probing their way slowly and deftly into the centre of your heart, with their kindly, nurturing ways.

Libra (cardinal air) pushes with such polite consideration and charm that only the most discerning of people will realise that the true aim of this cool sign is in the furthering of their own needs and desires. Diplomacy, tact and finesse are used in abundance by clever, unobtrusive Librans and in no time at all they achieve their purpose as others willingly lend a helping hand. They are usually respected for their harmonious dispositions.

Capricorn (cardinal earth) pushes with cautious, plodding, insidious deliberation. Basically passive and shy, like the Cancerian, they find it difficult to move to the front with any form of speed. They know what they want and are determined to achieve their aims, but often have to wait for an eternity before mustering the courage and confidence to make the most of their opportunities. Occasionally they can become ruthless in their objectives, using or abusing others in order to attain their goal. But patience is a word they truly understand.

Summary: Cardinal signs represent push, drive, self-assertiveness. Everybody needs a little Cardinal incentive in their lives. A lack of this quadruplicity in the birth chart can indicate a person who is forever waiting in the background for good fortune to drop in his lap, but without the initial ardour and enthusiasm to succeed he will usually flounder. Too much Cardinality in the birthchart can produce an extremely self-centred individual with little sensitivity to the feelings of others. It is worth noting, however, that these people will be stridently assertive for the benefit of those whom they care about too.

FIXED

Fixed signs live up to their name. They can be tremendously set in their ways and stubborn to the point of stupidity. Too much of this grouping in a birth chart can cause self-induced ruts, lack of direction in life, and a problem in adjusting to changing circumstances. On the other hand they are loyal, tenacious, dedicated and highly capable, with a remarkably good business acumen and executive streak. When strongly fixed individuals decide that another person is worthy of their esteem, they can also be remarkably generous, and supportive. Adamant, egocentric and unchanging, however, they often suffer more than the other groupings when trauma or difficulties occur in their lives. All the fixed signs will hang on with grim determination to everything they value in life.

Taurus (fixed earth). This sign is the most accumulative in materialistic issues. Financial status and worldly possessions represent security to the stolid, but passive Taurean. You will therefore rarely find an extremely poor individual born under this sign – their persistent, tenacious natures stand them in good stead. Once these people decide upon a course of action (often after extreme deliberation) nothing on earth will deter them. Fixed earth is exactly as it sounds – strong and unyielding even under a muddy surface.

Leo (fixed fire). Leo's flames burn steadily and brightly. This sign too is unyielding but not so much with possessions and belongings as with their own resources, their egos and their creativity. If this sign decides to rear itself up from its lazy behind (think of the male Lion sleeping all day!) then the heights they can achieve through sheer strength of character, determination and talent are remarkable. However, they do expect a just reward for their painstaking efforts – and nothing suits this vain, but likeable sign, better than being worshipped and idolised by their multitude of followers. Financial remuneration falls a poor second to their love of being loved! It is important to remember, however, that it is extremely difficult to put out a Leo fire once it has been started.

Scorpio (fixed water). The still, deep waters of huge lakes describe very aptly the qualities of this intensely emotional fixed sign. Scorpio people will hang on to their feelings – love, jealousy, hate, power, possessiveness, until the bitter end. The problem is that the deep water of these beautiful lakes cannot go anywhere. It remains still and stagnant underneath, unlike the swirling oceans of Cancer and the flowing rivers of Pisces. Scorpio emotions, therefore, are usually held in check. They possess all the tenacity, and determination of the other fixed signs, but it their feelings and emotions which are the crucial point of their extreme perseverance.

Aquarius (fixed air). Strongly opinionated, utterly assured that they are correct, Aquarian people will always endeavour to convince others of the errors of their ways. This is the sign of fixed mental attitudes. Aquarians possess clever minds, friendly, sociable demeanours and unrivalled talent, but all too often they are overbearing in their dogmatic views. A strongly Aquarian individual will rarely see the other side of the coin, and this invariably leads to his downfall. In no time at all, however, these unusual individuals will be pursing yet another theme, humanitarian cause or creative talent to grace the world.

Summary: Fixed signs are stubborn, determined, tenacious, strong-willed, intense, steady, reliable, unmoving and sometimes boring because of their lack of flexibility. We all need some fixity in our birth charts however, because once having pushed ourselves to achieve our aims (Cardinal), we need the steadfastness to carry on. Planets situated in fixed signs render us with concentrative ability and continued stimulation in whatever we attempt. Without this grouping in our charts we would be rushing around willy nilly, getting nowhere.

MUTABLE

Mutable signs are essentially adaptable. They lack the drive of the cardinal signs and the dedication of the fixed signs, but they do possess an innate ability to change their way of life, if necessary. All too often, however, they are pulled in varying directions by stronger individuals than themselves. Generally speaking, these signs have speedy minds and learn easily, but they forget and lose interest quickly if not stimulated enough. They are the extreme antithesis of the fixed sign quadruplicity. All four mutable signs project their somewhat dissipated energy in a different manner, however:

Gemini (mutable air). Lively, versatile, extremely intelligent and quick-witted, Geminians tend to scatter their mental ability too much. They love learning or attempting to do anything which taxes their enquiring minds. They are interesting people who can talk their way into, or out of, any given situation, but they seldom stay around long enough to reap any long-standing rewards. Loyalty is definitely not their forté, so don't expect them to be around when you need them.

Virgo (mutable earth). Shifting, moving earth, is uncommon – only occasionally rearing its head in the form of earthquakes or other strange phenomena. It therefore stands to reason that Virgo is an extremely difficult sign to understand. They are restless in practical, down-to-earth, mundane matters and can become carping, critical and resentful when communication or movement is restricted. If pressurized too much they can surprise us with their tumultuous energy and ability to destroy. The subjects of this "Mercury-ruled" sign tend to use their mental attributes in a more practical manner than Geminians.

Sagittarius (mutable fire). The enthusiastic energy of this forthright sign continually changes direction. The fire of Sagittarius is swept this way and that, rarely stopping long enough to enable any form of concentrative energy to build up. More dynamic than the cool air sign of Gemini, Sagittarian people can fascinate us with their charm, wit, and outgoing manner. Their biggest problem is that they tend to exaggerate (remember the huge planet Jupiter rules this sign) – and almost anything can be blown up out of proportion. Do not rely upon them too heavily, therefore, to fulfil their promises. They truly mean what they say – when they say it, but come tomorrow all will be forgotten, as their flame of restless, changeable energy burns in a different direction.

Pisces (mutable water). This sign is renowned for its moody sensitivity. Changeable, flowing emotions, like a meandering river, aptly describes the Pisceans feelings. They can feel very strongly about something or someone one day, then totally averse to the object of their passion the following day. Never expect a Piscean to be constant. It is this very inconstancy that leads this sign to seek out all forms of escapism. But just as the river eventually flows out into the sea, the Piscean is capable of putting everything behind him and starting afresh. They learn through their feelings and intuition rather then by accepted standards.

Summary: Mutable signs are changeable, moody, versatile, lively, communicative, lacking in concentration and depth, multi-talented, intelligent, imaginative, unreliable. We all need a little of this quadruplicity within our birth chart to prevent us from stagnating and to keep us open to change. Too much mutability, however, can cause us to suffer from a never-ending stream of restless dilemmas. Never knowing which road to embark upon, strongly mutable people will often end up choosing the wrong path, sometimes straying by the wayside when it becomes obvious that their chosen course is unsuitable. Mutable people always crave stimulation of some kind. They are highly-strung individuals and it is therefore fortunate that they possess the adaptability to be able to cope with life's problems and seek out more fortuitous avenues.

Before moving on to the next lesson, try to absorb as much as you can about the different groupings of the signs, and answer the following questions as fully as possible.

1. List all the six negative signs using their symbols only.
2. Give the two alternative titles for the Active/Passive groupings.
3. Which element represents mental activity?
4. Name the three Fire signs (using symbols again).
5. Name some qualities of the cardinal quadruplicity.
6. In what manner does a Taurean person represent his fixity of character?
7. Name the mutable fire sign.
8. What does the element of water represent?
9. Which is the odd one out and why? Virgo, Taurus, Scorpio and Capricorn.
10. Name the seventh sign of the zodiac and it's three groupings.

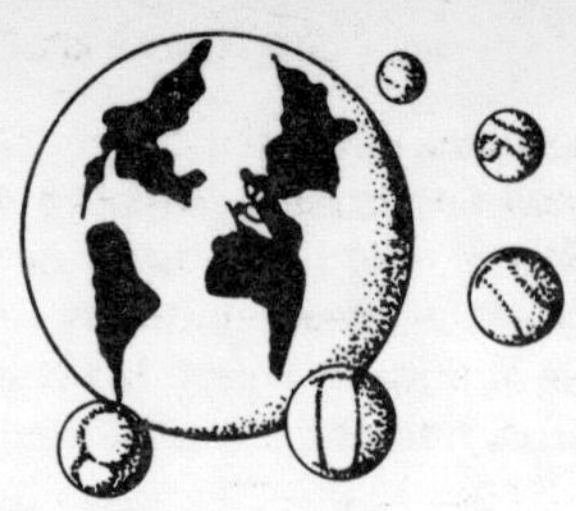

3 · Birth Chart Calculation

As mentioned in the Foreword, the calculation of a birth chart can often deter many would-be students from learning astrology. But you don't have to be a mathematical genius to learn how to erect a chart and derive pleasure from the process, especially with my system, which eliminates the outdated use of logarithms and detailed calculation which serve little purpose in interpretation. Nowadays, too, with the advent of calculators, computers and much pre-printed information, the erection of a birth chart is certainly a great deal easier than it was several hundred years ago.

You do, however, require the following items of stationery and books:

Planetary Ephemeris

These books list the daily positions of the planets. The most commonly available are as follows:

The Concise Planetary Ephemeris for the Years 1900 to 2000 (Noon Edition), available in paperback in two fifty-year sections.

The American Ephemeris for the Years 1900 to 2000 (Noon Edition), available in one paperback edition.

Raphael's Astronomical Ephemeris for the planets' places for each separate year.

Ideally, you should purchase either of the two complete editions mentioned above, ensuring that you acquire a Noon position edition rather than a Midnight edition as all the calculation in this book is based upon the position of the planets at noon. (There is a list of publishers and stockists in Appendix 3). If, however, you feel you would prefer to take the subject very slowly, commencing purely with the calculation of your own birth chart, then for economical reasons it would be better to purchase the single ephemeris for the year of your birth.

RAPHAEL'S TABLES OF HOUSES

Three small, inexpensive booklets commonly used in birth chart erection:

Tables of Houses for Great Britain
Tables of Houses for Northern Latitudes } Used solely for births
Tables of Houses for Southern Latitudes } outside Great Britain

ATLAS OR GAZETTEER

Either of the above would be suitable providing it lists the latitudes and longitudes of all the major towns in the world. It is relatively easy, however, to calculate longitude and latitude positions from maps.

BIRTH CHART FORMS

These are available from the stockists or my P.O. Box address as listed in Appendix 3.

OTHER USEFUL COMMODITIES

A calculator – for the less mathematically inclined. A pencil (do not use a pen in the initial stages), ruler and rubber – to draw up the birth chart.

If you are on a shoestring budget and only want to work out your own birth chart for the time being – providing you were born in or around London, or Liverpool, you could eliminate the use of the Tables of Houses for Great Britain, as the tables for these two cities are listed in all single editions of *Raphael's Astronomical Ephemeris*. If you were born in London, you could also manage without the atlas or gazetteer.

It can be extremely cheap to learn astrology, but for those students who wish to work out the birth charts of their friends and family a small outlay is required. Bearing all this in mind, astrology is still a remarkably economical subject to study.

EXAMPLES

Having spoken about the necessary tools we are now ready to commence with the calculation. For this we will use several fictitious examples increasing in complexity of calculation, as follows:

EXAMPLE 1 (involving minimum calculation)

Female: Born 22 February 1982, at 9.15 a.m., Lewisham, London.

Take a blank sheet of paper (or a birth chart form if available) and write on it the above details. The time of birth is extremely important – if you do not know the time of birth (within half an hour) then it is extremely difficult to erect a true blueprint of the character at birth.

We must now ensure that the time given is actual Greenwich Mean Time (the whole system of astrological calculation is based upon converting Greenwich Mean Time to Sidereal Time which is the true or *real* time derived from the orbits of the planets). If the birth occurred during British Summertime then we must deduct one hour from the birth time in order to arrive at Greenwich Mean Time. Certain years during the war adopted Double Summertime, necessitating a deduction of two hours and from February 1968 to the end of October 1971 British Standard Time was in operation – the clocks remaining one hour ahead of Greenwich Mean Time throughout the year, so that *all* births during these years require one hour to be deducted from their birth time. Appendix 1 lists the changing Summertimes from the year 1916 to the present day.

Our example female was born during winter hours and therefore her birth time of 9.15 a.m. is actual Greenwich Mean Time.

We can now proceed onto the longitude and latitude, but as the birth occurred extremely close to Greenwich no calculation is necessary. (Many London births contain only minimal degrees of longitude due to their close proximity to Greenwich, thereby necessitating very little geographical adjustment.) Towns in the Outer London boroughs, such as Surrey, Middlesex, Essex, etc., should always be included in the longitude, latitude adjustment.

Now, turn to the copy of the relevant page from *Raphael's*

Astronomical Ephemeris for the year 1982 on page 130. You will note that in the column adjacent to 22 February (on the right-hand side) there is another column, marked Sidereal Time. This is the *true* astronomical time at noon, and is listed as 22 hours, 8 minutes and 15 seconds. The next step is to ascertain the sidereal time for the actual time of birth. (For a person lucky enough to have been born at midday, the following calculation is not necessary.) Depending upon whether the birth occurred during the morning or the afternoon you will need either to subtract or to add to the given sidereal time at noon. Our example was born at 9.15 a.m., thus indicating that we should *subtract* from the time as follows:

H	M	S
22	08	15
-2	45	00
19	23	15

(Remember that 9.15 a.m. is actually 2 hours 45 minutes *before* noon, but a birth occurring at 9.15 p.m. would necessitate an addition of 9 hours, 15 minutes to the sidereal time. For those of you whose mathematics are a little rusty, do not forget that we are dealing with *time*: 60 seconds to the minute, 60 minutes to the hour, and 24 hours in a day.)

We now have a new sidereal time, but one more slight adjustment is required before we can say this is the actual sidereal time at birth. This is called the *acceleration on the interval*, and is necessary because sidereal time is actually fractionally faster than Greenwich Mean Time – a sidereal day is completed almost four minutes faster than a Mean Time day. The calculation for this adjustment is extremely easy, however, and if accidentally omitted from a birth chart it will not radically alter the final result.

To calculate the acceleration on the interval you must allow *10 seconds* for every hour of difference in time, before or from noon. Our example has a difference of 2 hours 45 minutes, giving an acceleration figure of 27 seconds to be deducted from the above worked out sidereal time:

H	M	S	
19	23	15	- Acceleration on interval
		27	(10 secs. per hr)
19	22	48	

Remember always to put this figure in the seconds column (or minutes and seconds if the result is above sixty seconds). The maximum amount of acceleration in any calculation is only two minutes – an extremely small amount, but it would drastically alter the chart if it were placed in the wrong column(s)!

Having arrived at the new sidereal time of 19 22 48 we should now look at the longitude figure. In this first example, however, there is no longitude to calculate as the child was born close to Greenwich. No other adjustments being required, we have therefore reached the sidereal time for this child at her time of birth.

From this figure we are able to find out the Ascendant, (Rising Sign – see Lesson 7) which rules the personality structure of the child, and erect the personal birth chart. Turn to the copy of the Table of Houses for London (Latitude 51 degrees 32 minutes North) in Appendix 5, and look down the column marked Sidereal Time until you find the nearest figure to our time of 19 22 48, which is 19 22 18. Look across (to the right) to the column marked 'Ascen' and you will find the figure of 14 degrees, 35 minutes. Glancing upwards you will find the glyph (symbol) for the sign of Taurus situated half way down the column. This is the Ascending sign. Glancing across to the left under the column marked 10 (next to the Sidereal Time section) you will see the figure 19 which means nineteen degrees. Glancing upwards, underneath the number 10 there is the symbol for the sign of Capricorn. This sign is the Midheaven – the highest point in the birth chart – an extremely important part of astrology, the meaning of which will be explained in Lesson 8.

We have so far thus calculated that our Example's Ascendant is 14 degrees 35 minutes in the sign of Taurus, with her Midheaven at 19 degrees in the sign of Capricorn. From this information we are able to erect the birth chart as detailed in Lesson 4. Before we move on to this lesson, however, it is important that you grasp the principles of calculation and for that several more examples of a slightly more complex nature are required.

EXAMPLE 2 (a more involved example, using Summertime and Longitude)

Male, born 6 July 1941 at 11.40 p.m. in Liverpool.

Using the same procedure as in the previous example, write down the above details on plain paper or a chart form. The birth time as given, is 11.40 p.m., but upon checking our Summertime list in Appendix

1, we find that during World War Two, Double Summertime was in operation from 4 May to 10 August, thereby necessitating a deduction of two hours to make the time of birth 9.40 p.m. Greenwich Mean Time.

Turn to the reproduction of *Raphael's Astronomical Ephemeris* for the year 1941 in Appendix 4, and for the date 6 July you will note that the sidereal time at noon is 6 56 18. Because our subject's birth occurred in the afternoon, we need to add on the difference from noon, thus:

H	M	S
6	56	18
+9	40	00
16	36	18

Now we deal with the acceleration on the interval, which is also added on due to the p.m. birth. (Remember to allow 10 seconds per hour, which means 5 seconds per half-hour, 2-3 for every quarter of an hour.) In this case, 9 hours 40 minutes difference results in an acceleration of approximately 97 seconds = 1 minute 37 seconds:

16	36	18
+	01	37
16	37	55

Because our subject was born in Liverpool we need to work out a slight longitude adjustment. After checking in our atlas/gazetteer we find that the longitude for Liverpool is 2 degrees 58 minutes West. We should write this figure in the appropriate section on the chart form or after the date and time of birth on a sheet of paper.

To calculate the longitude equivalent we must multiply the longitude figure by 4, the result, depending upon the size of the longitude, being in hours, minutes and seconds. A small longitude as in the case of Liverpool is relatively easy to work out:

2 degrees 58 minutes ×4
= 11 minutes 52 seconds.

This figure must now be added or subtracted from the calculated sidereal time. If the longitude is east of Greenwich you must *add* the resulting figure – if it is west of Greenwich you must *subtract* the figure. Liverpool is west of Greenwich so we must *subtract* the resulting 11 minutes 52 seconds:

	H	M	S
	16	37	55
–		11	52
	16	26	03

This is the final adjustment and therefore the true sidereal time at *birth* of the subject of our example.

We must now check through the Table of Houses for Liverpool (Latitude 53 degrees 25 minutes North) as reproduced in Appendix 5 to find the nearest sidereal time. You will notice beneath the 'Ascen' column that 16 26 03 falls midway between the sidereal times of 16 24 55 and 16 29 10:

16 24 55	=	6 degrees 58 minutes	Aquarius rising
16 29 10	=	8 degrees 46 minutes	Aquarius rising

Logically therefore, as our calculated time falls midway between the two so must the Ascendant – giving us a figure of 7 degrees 54 minutes. (If you find this difficult or confusing, then use a calculator.) We need not worry about the minutes involved in this sum – the 7 degrees is more than enough to base a good interpretation upon (remember my comments in the foreword about the lack of completely accurate data concerning the time of birth).

So we have arrived at an Ascendant of 7 degrees Aquarius for our male subject. Looking across to find the Midheaven degree we find it falls midway between 8 and 9 degrees of Sagittarius, thereby giving us a figure of 8 and a half degrees (8 degrees 30 minutes), but the figure of 8 degrees will suffice.

In Lesson 4 we will erect our subject's birth chart using the following calculations:

Ascendant 7 degrees Aquarius
Midheaven 8 degrees Sagittarius

EXAMPLE 3 (A slightly more complex birth in England using Summertime and Longitude)

Female: Born 24 October 1963, 11.05 p.m in Canterbury, Kent.

Upon checking our Summertime tables we find that the above date was still within Summertime and therefore requires one hour to be deducted, giving a Greenwich Mean Time birth of 10.05 p.m.

The sidereal time at *noon* is 14 08 41, to which we must *add* the difference from noon, which is 10 hours, 5 minutes:

H	M	S
14	08	41
+10	05	00
24	13	41

The next step is to *add* on the acceleration on the interval of 10 hours 5 minutes, which results in 101 seconds – 1 minute 41 seconds:

24	13	41
+	01	41
24	15	22

Now we deal with the longitude. Upon checking our atlas or gazetteer we find that Canterbury has a longitude of 1 degree 05 minutes *east* of Greenwich, which means we must *add* on the longitude equivalent which amounts to 04M 20S.

H	M	S
24	15	22
+	04	20
24	19	42

In this case, however, this is not the final sidereal time. Because we are dealing with a 24-hour time-system, any sidereal time exceeding the twenty-four hours as in the above example must have a full twenty-four hours deducted from the figure:

24	19	42
−24	00	00
00	19	42

This then, is the local sidereal time at birth for our subject. The closest figure to this in our Table of Houses for London (if you possess the Table of Houses booklet you will notice that the Table of Houses for Taunton, Latitude 51 degrees 1 minute North, is equally usable, being fractionally closer to Canterbury's latitude than London) is 00 18 21. Looking down the 'Ascen' column, we find a figure of 29 degrees 55 minutes in the sign of Cancer, but as the above sidereal time is in fact a little over the figure of 00 18 21, and the ascending degree at this figure has almost reached 0 degrees of Leo, we can safely assume that our above example will actually have 0 degrees of Leo on her Ascendant, rather than 29 degrees of Cancer. Looking across to the left to the column marked 10 we see that the Midheaven degree will be approximately 5½ degrees of Aries, but 5 degrees will suffice.

In Lesson 4 we will erect this subject's birth chart using the following:

Ascendant 0 degrees Leo
Midheaven 5 degrees Aries

EXAMPLE 4

Male: Born 12 January 1970 at 12.30 p.m. in Glasgow, Scotland.

When checking our Summertime tables we find that 1970 was a year during which British Standard Time was in operation and therefore one hour should be deducted for any birth during this year.

After deducting one hour from example, we arrive at a birthtime of 11.30 a.m. Greenwich Mean Time. In the relevant reproduction for January 1970 from *Raphael's Astronomical Ephemeris*, in Appendix 4, we find that the sidereal time for noon on 12 January is 19 26 16. From this figure we need to deduct the 30 minutes interval *to* noon:

H	M	S
19	26	16
–	30	00
18	56	16

The Acceleration on the Interval *to* noon is minimal: 5 seconds only. For practice purposes we will deduct this amount, but its omission would make no difference at all to the final figure.

18	56	16
–		05
18	56	11

Next we turn to Glasgow's longitude, which is 4 degrees 16 minutes West of Greenwich which after multiplying by four results in 17 minutes 04 seconds to be *subtracted* from the above sidereal time.

H	M	S
18	56	11
–	17	04
18	39	07

This then is the sidereal time for the birth. Turning to the Tables of Houses for Glasgow (Latitude 55 degrees 53 minutes North) shown in Appendix 5) we find that the nearest sidereal time to our figure is 18 39 11, the Ascendant being 28 degrees 14 minutes of the sign Aries, and the Midheaven 9 degrees of Capricorn.

Ascendant 28 degrees Aries
Midheaven 9 degrees Capricorn

The chart will be erected in Lesson 4.

EXAMPLE 5 (A foreign birth in the Northern Hemisphere)

Male: Born 2 October 1963 at 9.23 p.m. in New York.

All countries other than Great Britain use their own zone standard time which must be converted into Greenwich mean time. Some atlases and gazetteers may show zone time-differences, or you may be able to find out the information from your local library, from an airport, or from the appropriate embassy. Margaret Hone's *Modern Text Book of Astrology* contains a fairly comprehensive list of overseas countries' Standard Times.

New York, is five hours behind us, and does keep Summertime. (Many countries do not keep Summertime, and therefore require no adjustment.) We must therefore *add* five hours onto the time of birth, giving us a time of 2.23 a.m. *3 October 1963* (notice we have moved on a day in this country). The one hour Summertime must now be deducted to arrive at the time of 1.23 a.m. Greenwich Mean Time. *All our calculation from now on is based on the time 1.23 a.m. 3 October 1963.*

The sidereal time at noon on this day (check with the copy of *Raphael's Astronomical Ephemeris* for October 1963) shown in Appendix 4, is 12 45 53. From this time we need to *deduct* the amount of interval, which is 10 hours 37 minutes to noon:

H	M	S
12	45	53
−10	37	00
02	08	53

We now also deduct the accleration on the interval, which amounts to 109 seconds = 1 minute 49 seconds

02	08	53
–	01	49
02	07	04

Then we move on to the longitude conversion. New York is 74 degrees West of Greenwich which, converted to time = 4 hours 56 minutes. This difference must now be *subtracted* from the above sidereal time:

H	M	S
02	07	04
−04	56	00
21	11	04

You will note from the above calculation that 24 hours has been added on to the initial 2 hours of sidereal time in order to subtract the 4 hours 56 minutes.

We have now arrived at the actual sidereal time at birth for our American subject, and can turn to the appropriate Tables of Houses – those for New York (Latitude 40 degrees 40 minutes North), shown in Appendix 5. The sidereal time of 21 11 04 is midway between 21 09 53 and 21 13 52. The Ascendant should therefore fall midway between the two figures of 9 degrees 23 minutes of the sign Gemini and 10 degrees 28 minutes of Gemini, which produces a figure of approximately 9 degrees 56 minutes. A rounded-up figure of 10 degrees of Gemini will be sufficient for the Ascending degree. Glancing left to the column marked 10, we find 15 degrees of Aquarius on the Midheaven.

Our American example therefore possesses:

Ascendant 10 degrees Gemini
Midheaven 15 degrees Aquarius

For a birth occurring in the Southern Hemisphere (for example, Australia), the same formula is followed as for a Northern Hemisphere birth until the local (final) sidereal time is reached, whereupon a further 12 hours must be added on. The Table of Houses for Southern Latitudes is then required in order to find the Ascendant and Midheaven. Once these have been found, the two signs are reversed to arrive at the final result. For instance, if the Ascendant were found to be 11 degrees Libra and the Midheaven 15 degrees Cancer, the reversal would make 11 degrees of Aries the Ascendant, and 15 degrees of Capricorn the Midheaven.

Southern Hemisphere calculation is a little more complex and should not really be attempted until you have mastered the calculation of British charts.

Before the questions here are some important points to remember when calculating the Ascendant and Midheaven positions in a birth chart.

1. Always write the full details down, preferably on a birth chart form.
2. Remember to use the appropriate Table of Houses for the nearest equivalent latitude.
3. When the local sidereal time amounts to more than 24 hours, always subtract 24 hours. Likewise, if need be, when the hours column is too large to be deducted from the other, always add 24 hours on to the sum you are subtracting from.
4. A birth occurring in the very early hours of the morning in Great Britain can sometimes go back to the preceding day if there are one or two hours of Summertime to be deducted. *Always* calculate the birth chart from the actual Greenwich Mean Time arrived at after the deduction of Summertime.
5. Acceleration on the interval is 10 seconds per hour and can only be a maximum of 2 minutes in any given day. Do not make the mistake of placing this in the hours column.
6. The longitude figure is always multiplied by 4, the answer being in hours, minutes and seconds. East of Greenwich longitudes are always *added* on, whilst West of Greenwich longitudes are always *subtracted*.

1. If somebody were born on 20 March 1976, would you deduct Summertime?
2. The longitude for Leeds, Yorkshire is 1 degree 32 minutes West. Convert this into minutes and seconds.
3. If you calculated a local sidereal time of 30 08 21 what would you need to do next?
4. What is the acceleration on the interval for somebody born at 4.00 a.m?
5. Looking at the example from *Raphael's Ephemeris* for July 1941 (Appendix 4) what is the sidereal time for Friday 11 July?
6. In the Tables of Houses for London (Appendix 5), what would the Ascendant and Midheaven be if the sidereal time was 13 09 53?
7. Complete the following sidereal time calculation:

H	M	S
05	16	21
−07	32	16

8. Looking at the Tables of Houses for London (Appendix 5), find out where 12 degrees 13 minutes of Virgo is ascending and give the appropriate sidereal time and Midheaven.
9. Complete the calculation below:

H	M	S
15	59	42
+07	14	28

10. From the Tables of Houses for Liverpool, what are the Ascendant and Midheaven if the sidereal time is:

16 06 58?

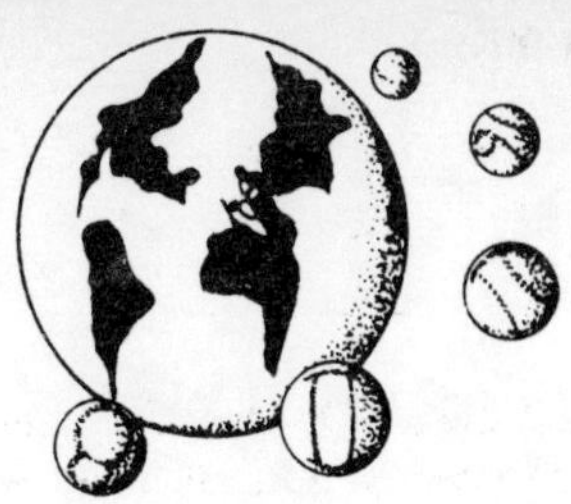

4 · Birth Chart Erection

In this lesson we are going to erect the five birth charts calculated in Lesson 3. This process is much easier if you have a blank chart form.

Example 1

Female: Born 22 February 1982 at 9.15 a.m., Lewisham, London. Ascendant 14 degrees Taurus, Midheaven 19 degrees Capricorn.

Using a blank chart form (or drawing your own circle of 360 degrees) the first task is to place the calculated Ascendant into the correct position, which is *always* on the left-hand side of the circle (see Diagram 1, page 30). Counting each dividing outer ring segment as 0 degrees count *down* (in an anticlockwise direction) to 14 degrees and place a short line or dot at this position. You will notice that each of the twelve segments is divided into 30 degrees (the number of degrees for each sign of the zodiac) and further divided into 5-degree sections. Place another dot or line at the next 14 degree section and the next until you have placed 12 marks in the circle, as in Diagram 1. A word of advice here. If the Ascendant is calculated between 0 and 15 degrees (of any sign) then it is better to count down from the central left 0 degree segment as per our example, but if the Ascendant is calculated to be between 16 and 29 degrees of a sign then it is neater and more readable to place the degree of Ascendant by counting *upwards* in clockwise direction from the central segment

DIAGRAM 1

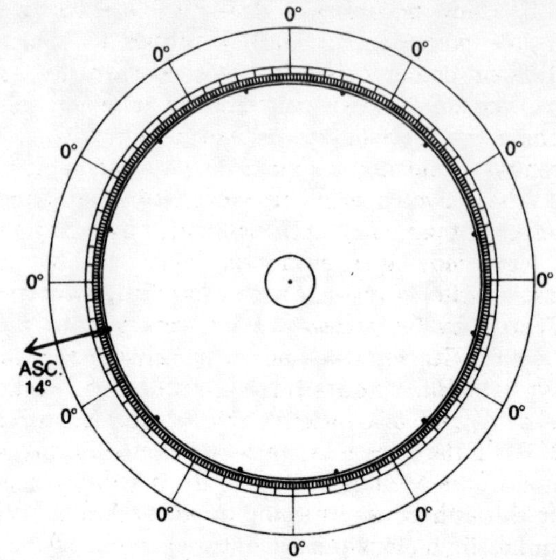

DIAGRAM 2

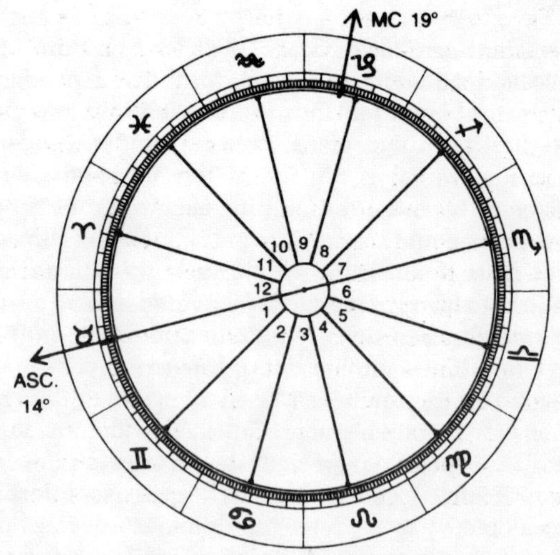

divider. (Example 4, with an Ascendant of 28 degrees Aries, Diagram No 7, shown on page 37, uses this direction.)

It is now necessary to draw twelve equal segments from the 14 degree position and mark in either by means of an arrow or different coloured pencil, the Ascendant and its degree, as shown in Diagram 2. Then commencing with the segment immediately under the fourteen-degree Ascendant write in close to the small central circle, the numbers one to twelve as shown in Diagram 2. These twelve segments are called *houses* and are an extremely important part of chart interpretation as explained in Lesson 7.

Now, moving in an anticlockwise direction again, in the outer circle write in the signs of the zodiac, commencing with the sign Taurus, by the arrowed Ascendant, moving in sequence through Gemini, Cancer, Leo, and so on, always remembering to write in symbols. Having done this, we should then enter in the Midheaven, at 19 degrees of Capricorn, with a short arrow (check with Diagram 2). With the system of house division which we are learning, Equal House, the Midheaven must fall in either the eighth, ninth, tenth or eleventh house, the ninth and tenth being the most commonly found. If you arrive at any other position, then you have made an error somewhere and should check your calculations.

We are now ready to place in the circle the ten planets described in Lesson 1.

Turn to Appendix 4, where our copy of *Raphael's Ephemeris* for the month of February 1982 is shown, and find on your immediate left-hand side Monday 22 February. The *second* column along from this date shows us the position of the Sun at noon, which is 3 degrees 32 minutes in the sign of Pisces (note the change from Aquarius to Pisces on 19 February). As the Sun moves one degree per day, and therefore 30 minutes every twelve hours (half a day), 15 minutes every six hours, and 7 and a half minutes every three hours, we now have to ascertain whether our subject, born at 9.15 a.m., two and three-quarters hours *before* midday, still has the Sun situated at 3 degrees of Pisces. The time differential in this instance shows that the Sun is situated at approximately six minutes *less* than 3 degrees 32 minutes – that is, at 3 degrees 26 minutes. Three degrees of Pisces then is the position of the Sun in our example's chart. Find this position on your chart form and write in the symbol for the Sun, with the relevant degrees as shown in Diagram 3 on page 33.

Next, we place the Moon into position on the chart form, using a similar procedure. Move across to the fourth column on the February

1982 ephemeris, marked Long. at the top, where you will see that the position of the Moon at *noon* on this day is 17 degrees 3 minutes Aquarius. The Moon is the swiftest-moving planet, completing its cycle in 28 days, and therefore one sign (one-twelfth) of the zodiac in approximately two and a half days. Using this calculation we can deduce that the Moon moves approximately one degree every two hours. *This formula is very important to remember*, as unless a person is born at noon, the degrees of the Moon according to the time of birth, are going to be slightly different to those stated in the ephemeris. The calculation is minimal and easy to work out in your head, but you can always use a calculator if necessary. Our subject, therefore, born at 9.15 a.m., two and three-quarter hours before noon, should have a Moon movement of almost one and a half degrees (around 1 degree 27 minutes). *Deduct* this figure from 17 degrees 3 minutes and you arrive at 15 degrees 36 minutes. We need not concern ourselves with the minutes at this stage as they are not pertinent to the general interpretation of a birth chart, and can now place the Moon in the birth chart at 15 degrees of Aquarius (see Diagram 3). Do remember, as with the calculation of the Ascendant that for any time *after* noon, addition will need to be used, and for any time *before* noon, subtraction.

Moving across to the right-hand side of our ephemeris page, ignoring all the remaining figures for the Moon, we arrive at the position of the planet Mercury at noon: 7 degrees 3 minutes of the sign Aquarius. You may notice at this stage, further up this column the letter D, which is short for *Direct* and the symbol ℞ which means *Retrograde*. When a planet is listed as Retrograde it appears from Earth to be moving in a backward motion. Once it begins to move forward again the Direct symbol is used as an indication. The interpretation of a retrograde planet is shown in Lesson 8. The Retrograde symbol should always be entered into the birth chart, if applicable. (Note in Diagram 3 that the planets Mars, Saturn and Pluto are all in Retrograde position.) The planet Mercury moves at a variable speed, sometimes moving only a few minutes per day and at others moving as much as 2 degrees per day. Its speed of motion can easily be ascertained by glancing at the previous day's position and then at the following day. On 22 February 1982, we can see that Mercury is not even moving 1 degree a day. From noon on 21 February to noon on the 22nd it has moved only 47 minutes. As you can see, however, at noon on the 22nd it has only just reached 7 degrees and 3 minutes. On

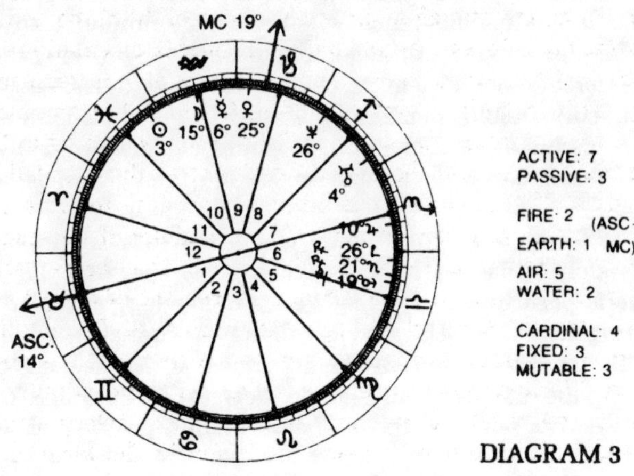

DIAGRAM 3

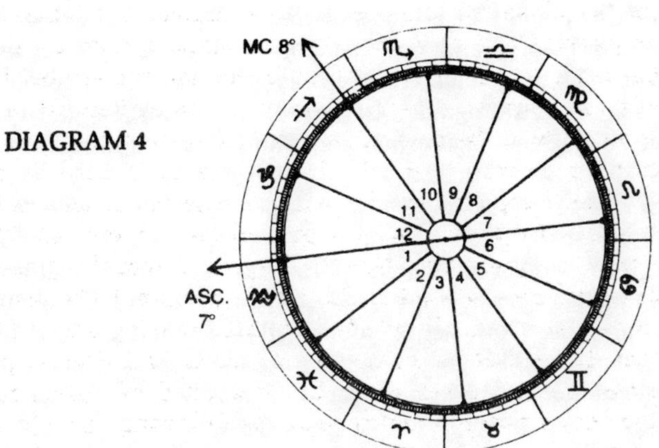

DIAGRAM 4

the assumption of the planet moving 47 minutes over twenty-four hours, it will move approximately 6 minutes over three hours (a calculator may be required here), and therefore, the two and three-quarter hour time-difference will necessitate around 5 to 6 minutes being deducted from the noon figures, thereby making the position of Mercury at 9.15 a.m. to be approximately 6 degrees 58 minutes. Mercury should therefore be written in the chart form as 6 degrees Aquarius as in Diagram 3. It would not matter greatly, however, if 7 degrees were written in, as the final figure is so close.

Now on to Venus – another planet which moves at a variable speed, but rarely as fast as Mercury when at its speediest. From our ephemeris page we can see that Venus is moving particularly slowly during February. (Usually it will travel through a whole sign in less than thirty days.) As it stands at 25 degrees of Capricorn on the 21st and still at 25 degrees of this sign on the 22nd, we can safely write in Venus at this position as in Diagram 3.

Mars can spend as long as six months in one sign, and only occasionally requires any further calculation from its noon position. On 22 February 1982, Mars is moving extremely slowly and has just gone retrograde (on 21 February). Its position therefore is 19 degrees Libra, as stated in the Ephemeris. Place this in your birth chart form as shown in Diagram 3.

The remaining planets are all too slow-moving to make any degree adjustments necessary, and are therefore written on the chart form as listed in the ephemeris: Jupiter at 10 degrees Scorpio; Saturn at 21 Libra, retrograde; Uranus at 4 degrees Sagittarius; Neptune at 26 degrees Sagittarius; and Pluto at 26 degrees Libra, retrograde.

Our birth chart is now complete with Ascendant, Midheaven and all ten planets listed.

The next step is to list on the chart form or on a sheet of paper the division of the planetary positions into Active and Passive, Elements and Quadruplicities. These listings alone will give remarkable insight into the character of the subject. As there are ten planets within the chart, each division must add up to ten. In Example 1, the following applies.

Active/Passive

Active (Positive)	7	(Moon, Mercury, Mars, Saturn, Uranus, Neptune and Pluto)

Passive: (Negative)	3	(Sun, Venus and Jupiter)

Elements

Fire	2	(Uranus and Neptune)
Earth	1	(Venus)
Air	5	(Moon, Mercury, Mars, Saturn and Pluto)
Water	2	(Sun and Jupiter)

Then add the Ascendant and Midheaven (*Medium Coeli*, MC for short) elements to the total. In this instance both are in Earth, extending the Earth element total to 3. (Note how this is entered in Diagram 3.)

Quadruplicities

Cardinal	4	(Venus, Mars, Saturn and Pluto)
Fixed	3	(Moon, Mercury and Jupiter)
Mutable	3	(Sun, Uranus and Neptune)

EXAMPLE 2

Male: Born 6 July 1941 at 11.40 p.m. (9.40. p.m. GMT) in Liverpool. Ascendant 7 degrees Aquarius. Midheaven 8 degrees Sagittarius.

Adopting the same procedure as in Example 1, first mark out each 7 degree section, and then draw up the house lines (these are called cusps and will be referred to as such from now on). Write in the house numbers, the Ascending sign and degree and the remaining signs in order on the chart wheel. Lastly mark in the Midheaven. At this stage the form should appear as in Diagram 4.

Next, turn to the relevant extract from *Raphael's Ephemeris* for the year 1941 (Appendix 5) and find the position of the Sun at noon in the second column along from the left marked 'Sun Long', which is 14 degrees of Cancer exactly. As our subject was born at 9.40 p.m. Greenwich Mean Time we would need to *add* minutes on to this degree, amounting to approximately 24 minutes, thereby making the position of the Sun 14 degrees 24 minutes. Fourteen degrees alone will suffice and should be entered in the birth chart (as shown in Diagram 5).

Looking across to the Moon's longitude column (fourth) we find a noon position of 12 degrees 5 minutes Sagittarius, which necessitates the *addition* (remember this is a p.m. birth) of several degrees to be

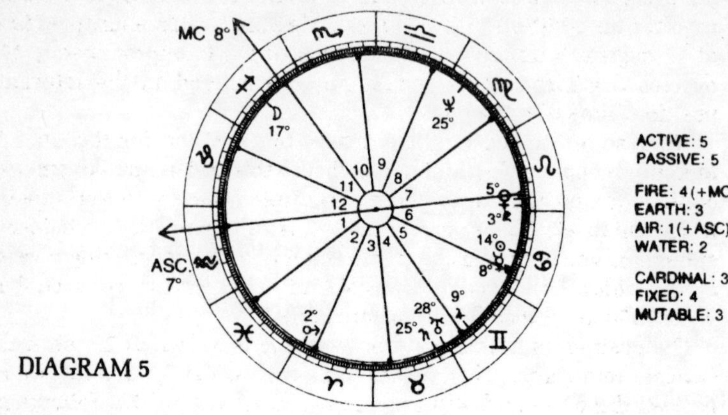

DIAGRAM 5

DIAGRAM 6

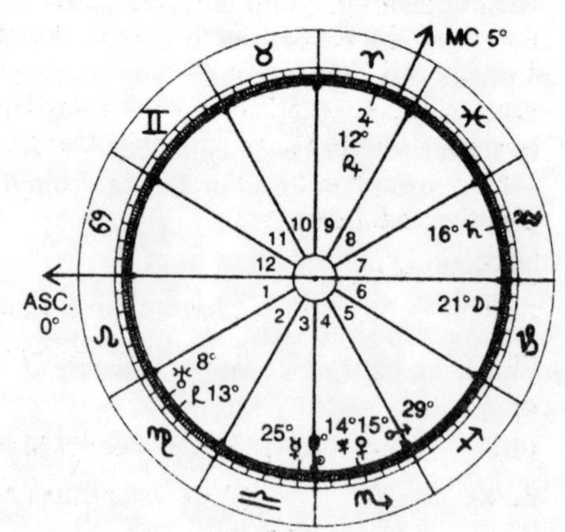

correct for the birth time of 9.40 p.m. Using our formula of one degree for every two hours we find that 9 hours 40 minutes *from* noon requires an addition of just under 5 degrees to our noon position of 12 degrees 5 minutes, thereby increasing it to approximately 17 degrees Sagittarius. This should now be entered in the relevant position (shown in Diagram 5).

Work across to the far right where the position for the planet Mercury is shown. You will notice that in this and earlier ephemeris editions the positioning of the planets from Mercury to Neptune is from right to left. Check your symbols carefully therefore in whatever ephemeris you may be using. Pluto is not listed in earlier single-year ephemerides. Abbreviated details of Pluto's movements between the years 1900 to 1980 are listed in Appendix 2.

The position of Mercury at noon on July is 8 degrees 28 minutes Cancer, retrograde. This means that the planet is moving in a backward motion and will remain at 8 degrees until the following day. Enter Mercury into the chart as shown in Diagram 5.

Venus is listed at 4 degrees 52 minutes in the sign of Leo and moving fairly quickly (note it has travelled 1 degree, 13 minutes since the previous day). It is therefore logical to presume that Venus will have reached well over 5 degrees of Leo at the birthtime of 9.40 p.m., and should be entered into the chart at this degree (Diagram 5).

Mars is at 2 degrees 27 minutes of Aries at noon, and not moving fast enough for any adjustment, so enter 2 degrees into the chart. Jupiter is at 9 degrees of Gemini. Saturn is at 24 degrees 58 minutes of Taurus at noon and therefore requires a rare adjustment as it will *just* reach 25 degrees Taurus by 9.40 p.m. Uranus is at 28 degrees of Taurus, and Neptune at 25 degrees Virgo. Check Appendix 2 to find Pluto's degree on 6 July 1941 – 3 degrees of Leo, and enter all these positions into the chart, to complete the wheel, as in Diagram 5.

Now we can enter the Active/Passive ratio, Elements and Quadruplicities as follows.

Active/Passive

Active	5	(Moon, Venus, Mars, Jupiter and Pluto)
Passive	5	(Sun, Mercury, Saturn, Uranus and Neptune)

Elements

Fire	4 (+MC)	(Moon, Venus, Mars and Pluto)
Earth	3	(Saturn, Uranus and Neptune)
Air	1 (+ASC)	(Jupiter)
Water	2	(Sun and Mercury)

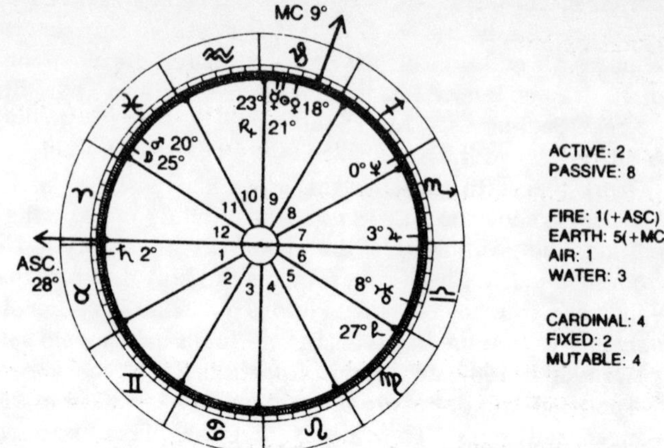

DIAGRAM 7

DIAGRAM 8

ACTIVE: 5
PASSIVE: 5

FIRE: 2
EARTH: 3
AIR: 3(+ASC/MC)
WATER: 2

CARDINAL: 4
FIXED: 3
MUTABLE: 3

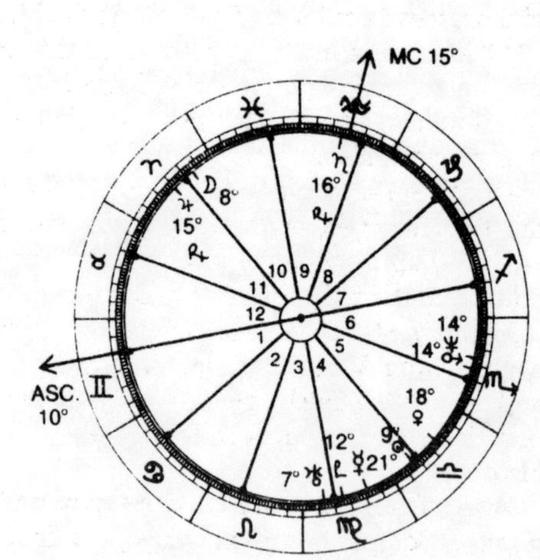

Quadruplicities

Cardinal	3	(Sun, Mercury and Mars)
Fixed	4	(Venus, Saturn, Uranus and Pluto)
Mutable	3	(Moon, Jupiter and Neptune)

(All the above are detailed in Diagram 5.)

EXAMPLE 3

Female: Born 24 October 1963, 11.05 p.m. (10.05. GMT), Canterbury, Kent. Ascendant 0 degrees Leo, Midheaven 5 degrees Aries.

By now you should be a little more confident about erecting a birth chart. Try drawing in the house cusps, Ascendant, Midheaven, house numbers and the twelve signs in their appropriate sections without glancing at Diagram 7. The calculated Ascendant at exactly 0 degrees makes life a little easier here as there is no counting down (or up) in order to position the Ascendant or house cusps. Check with Diagram 6 before moving on to place the planets from the sample of October 1963 *Raphael's Ephemeris* (Appendix 4).

Then turning to the Sun sign column for noon, we find a position of 0 degrees 21 minutes Scorpio. As the birth occurred at 10.05. p.m. GMT an approximate amount of 25 minutes needs to be added to this figure, making a total of 0 degrees 46 minutes. The Sun should therefore be entered into the appropriate place in the birth chart for 0 degrees Scorpio.

The Moon at noon is at 16 degrees 24 minutes Capricorn. Using the 1 degree movement for every two hours, the Moon at 10.05 p.m. will be at approximately 21 degrees of Capricorn. (Remember we are *adding* on the 5 degrees due to the p.m. birth).

Mercury stands at 22 degrees 42 minutes of Libra (note the change from Virgo to Libra on the 11th of the month) at Noon, and is moving fairly quickly. It will therefore be safe to assume that it will have reached 23 degrees of Libra at the time of birth.

Venus is also moving fairly quickly and stands at 14 degrees 59 minutes Scorpio at midday. It will undoubtedly be at 15 degrees by 10.05 p.m.

Slower-moving Mars remains at 29 degrees of Scorpio. Jupiter is at 12 degrees Aries, retrograde. Saturn is at 16 degrees of Aquarius,

Uranus at 8 degrees of Virgo, Neptune at 14 degrees Scorpio and Pluto (see Appendix 2) is at 13 degrees Virgo.

After entering all these positions check with Diagram 6 to ensure you are correct. Then count up the positions of the planets in Active/Passive signs, the elements and the quadruplicities, as in the first two examples.

Active/Passive

Active	3	(Mercury, Jupiter and Saturn)
Passive	7	(Sun, Moon, Venus, Mars, Uranus, Neptune and Pluto)

Elements

Fire	1 (+ ASC. and MC)	(Jupiter)
Earth	3	(Moon, Uranus and Pluto)
Air	2	(Mercury and Saturn)
Water	4	(Sun, Venus, Mars and Neptune)

Quadruplicities

Cardinal	3	(Moon, Mercury and Jupiter)
Fixed	5	(Sun, Venus, Mars, Saturn and Neptune)
Mutable	2	(Uranus and Pluto)

EXAMPLE 4

Male: Born 12 January 1970 12.30 p.m. (11.30 a.m. GMT), Glasgow, Scotland. Ascendant 28 degrees Aries, Midheaven 9 degrees Capricorn.

Mark in the Ascendant and house cusps (remembering to count two degrees *upwards* from the central 0 degree point as in Diagram 8) and then write in the house numbers, signs, and Midheaven as in previous examples, checking with Diagram 7 after completion.

Turn to Appendix 4 for the relevant extract from *Raphael's Ephemeris* for January 1970 and position the planets, without referring to the diagram or the following text.

You should have arrived at the following calculations:

Sun 21 degrees Capricorn, Moon 25 degrees Pisces, Mercury 23 degrees Capricorn, retrograde, Venus 18 degrees Capricorn, Mars 20 degrees Pisces, Jupiter 3 degrees Scorpio, Saturn 2 degrees Taurus, Uranus 8 degrees Libra, Neptune 0 degrees Sagittarius, Pluto 27 degrees Virgo, retrograde.

Did you get them right? Only the Moon requires any adjustment, as the birth occurs within half an hour of midday.

Now count up the planets using the usual procedure, checking with Diagram 7, if unsure.

Active/Passive

Active 2 (Uranus and Neptune)
Passive 8 (Sun, Moon, Mercury, Venus, Mars, Jupiter, Saturn and Pluto)

Elements

Fire 1 (+ASC) (Neptune)
Earth 5 (+MC) (Sun, Mercury, Venus, Saturn and Pluto)
Air 1 (Uranus)
Water 3 (Moon, Mars and Jupiter)

Quadruplicities

Cardinal 4 (Sun, Mercury, Venus and Uranus)
Fixed 2 (Jupiter and Saturn)
Mutable 4 (Moon, Mars, Neptune and Pluto)

EXAMPLE 5

Male: Born 2 October 1963 at 9.23 p.m. (1.23 a.m. GMT 3 October 1963), in New York. Ascendant 10 degrees Gemini, Midheaven 15 degrees Aquarius.

Enter in all the relevant information before turning to the planets' positions. You should be far more competent by now, but refer to Diagram 8 if you feel unsure.

Then the planets. Remember, for calculation and planetary adjustment purpose, that we are dealing with a new date and time: 1.23 a.m. on *3 October 1963*. Try to write in the planets' degrees without any referral.

You should arrive at the following positions:

Sun 9 degrees Libra, Moon 8 degrees Aries, Mercury 21 Virgo, Venus 18 degrees Libra, Mars 14 degrees Scorpio, Jupiter 15 degrees Aries, retrograde, Saturn 16 degrees Aquarius, retrograde, Uranus 7 degrees Virgo, Neptune 14 degrees Scorpio and Pluto 12 degrees Virgo.

Count the planets in the three different groupings as usual.

Active/Passive

Active 5 (Sun, Moon, Venus, Jupiter and Saturn)
Passive 5 (Mercury, Mars, Uranus, Neptune and Pluto)

Elements
Fire 2 (Moon and Jupiter)
Earth 3 (Mercury, Uranus and Pluto)
Air 3 (+ ASC. and MC) (Sun, Venus and Saturn)
Water 2 (Mars and Neptune)

Quadruplicities
Cardinal 4 (Sun, Moon, Venus and Jupiter)
Fixed 3 (Mars, Saturn and Neptune)
Mutable 3 (Mercury, Uranus and Pluto)

Check the completed chart with Diagram 8.

Having completed the five examples you should now be in a position to attempt a great deal more by yourself. Use the following test to assess the level you have achieved. Do not attempt to move on to the next chapter until you have answered at *least* seven questions with 100 per cent accuracy.

1. If an Ascendant was calculated to be 20 degrees of any sign, would you count up or *down* from the central 0 degree point?
2. From the ephemeris page for February 1982, give the exact position (in degrees) for the Moon for a person born on 28 February at 6.00 a.m.
3. Using the same extract and date, assess how far (in degrees and minutes) the planet Mercury has moved between noon on 27 February to noon on 28 February.
4. What do the symbols ℞ and D mean in the ephemeris?
5. Name the date on which Mercury turns Direct in January 1970.
6. If the Moon is situated at 28 degrees of Pisces at noon on a given date state its position at 10.00 p.m. on the same day.
7. From the extract from the ephemeris for July 1941, give the date that Venus enters Virgo.
8. How long does it take the Sun to travel 1 degree?
9. Name the planet which is *usually* the fastest-moving after the Moon.
10. Place these chart positions into their relevant three groupings (Elements, etc.):

    Sun 9 degrees Sagittarius, Moon 12 degrees Aries, Mercury 22 degrees Sagittarius, Venus 20 degrees Capricorn, Mars 7 degrees Sagittarius, Jupiter 24 degrees Taurus, Saturn 16 degrees Leo, Uranus 9 degrees Scorpio, Neptune 13 degrees Sagittarius, Pluto 13 degrees Libra.

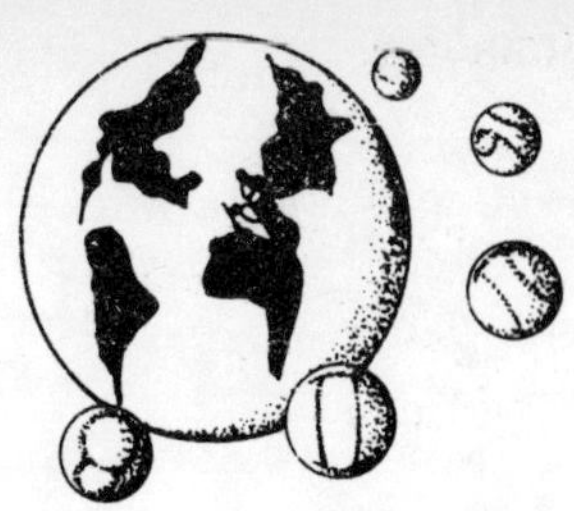

5 · Calculation of Aspects

We are now almost at the end of the calculation stage of a natal birth chart, but before moving on to the interpretation we need to learn about the *aspects* which the planets make with one another and the important impact these make upon our characters.

Because the zodiac wheel consists of 360 degrees divided into twelve sections of 30 degrees, the main aspects used by astrologers are those divisible by thirty, of which there are *seven*, as follows:

The Conjunction ☌

Any two (or more) planets positioned in the chart together, that is, within 8 degrees of one another, are said to be *conjunct* or *in conjunction*. The closer the planets, the more important the aspect becomes. For instance, if the planets Mars and Venus were both situated at 20 degrees of Libra they would be in exact conjunction with one another, but if Mars were at 20 degrees and Venus at either 28 degrees or 12 degrees of Libra they would still be in wide conjunction. The effect of this major aspect can be variable. A conjunction between the two complementary feminine planets Moon and Neptune energises refinement, delicacy and aesthetic ideals, whereas Moon conjuncting masculine, eccentric Uranus is a turbulent, stress-inducing combination.

Some examples of conjunctions occurring within the five birth charts used in Lessons 3 and 4 are:

Example 1 – Mars/Saturn/Pluto
Example 2 – Saturn/Uranus, Mercury/Sun, Pluto/Venus
Example 3 – Uranus/Pluto, Neptune/Venus, Sun/Mercury
Example 4 – Venus/Sun/Mercury, Mars/Moon
Example 5 – Uranus/Pluto, Mars/Neptune, Moon/Jupiter.

The conjunction is the easiest of the seven aspects to identify because the planets involved are always extremely close together and usually in the same sign. But be careful, a planet situated at 28 degrees of one sign can still be in conjunction with another at 6 degrees of the following sign.

THE SEMI-SEXTILE ⚺

This is a far less important aspect than the conjunction and involves two (or more) planets situated at a distance of 30 degrees apart. An orb of 2 degrees in either direction is allowable, so, for example, a planet at 10 degrees of Aries would be semi-sextile planets at 12 degrees of Taurus and 8 degrees of Pisces. The effect of this aspect is usually mildly favourable, but once again the temperament of the planets involved must be taken into account.

Some typical examples from our five subjects are:

Example 1 – Neptune–Venus
Example 2 – Jupiter–Mercury
Example 3 – Sun–Mars
Example 4 – None
Example 5 – Uranus–Sun

The semi-sextile aspect is relatively easy to identify, as the planets involved are nearly always situated one sign (or house) apart.

THE SEXTILE ✱

The Sextile involves two (or more) planets placed 60 degrees apart with an allowable orb of 4 degrees. For example, a planet at 12 degrees of Sagittarius would be sextile planets at 13 degrees of Aquarius and 8 degrees of Libra. The sextile can be one of the most beneficial aspects of all, as the planets involved are usually in signs which are elementally compatible, such as the fire sign Sagittarius with the air signs of Libra and Aquarius, or the earth sign Taurus with the water signs Pisces and Cancer. Air fans the flames of the fire, and earth contains the emotions of the water. This aspect, therefore, usually represents opportunities and optimism, or talents well utilised.

Some examples from our five subjects:

Example 1 – Pluto–Neptune, Uranus–Mercury
Example 2 – Jupiter–Venus
Example 3 – Pluto/Neptune–Venus, Saturn–Jupiter
Example 4 – Pluto–Neptune, Venus/Sun/Mercury–Mars, Sun/Mercury-Moon
Example 5 – Pluto/Mars–Neptune, Saturn–Jupiter

Try to recognise the sextile aspect by looking at the signs involved. If they are both active or both passive and the planets 56 to 64 degrees apart (using the 4 degree orb) then they must be forming a sextile.

THE SQUARE □

This is one of the major aspects and usually the most potent after the conjunction. It is formed by two (or more) planets situated 90 degrees apart, with an allowable 8 degree orb. For example, a planet at 17 degrees of Scorpio will be in square aspect with another at 17 degrees of Leo or another at 10 degrees of Aquarius, the former being an exact square aspect, the latter involving a 7 degree orb. Invariably a difficult, tension-motivated aspect, the square often causes much trouble within a birth chart, especially during the immature years. A square between two incompatible planets such as Jupiter and Saturn, usually causes more problems than one between two compatible planets such as the Sun and Jupiter. Square aspects can be utilised beneficially, but it takes time, patience and understanding.

Examples of squares in our five subjects' charts are:

Example 1 – Mars/Saturn/Pluto–Venus, Jupiter–Mercury Uranus–Sun
Example 2 – Mars-Mercury, Neptune–Moon
Example 3 – Moon-Mercury, Neptune/Venus–Saturn
Example 4 – None
Example 5 – Mars/Neptune–Saturn

For the beginner, squares are not always easy to identify. If, however, you have learnt the three groupings of the signs thoroughly, you will now be reaping the rewards. All the quadruplicities are in square aspect to one another. For example, planets in Aries may be square to planets in Capricorn or Cancer. Planets in Virgo may be square to any situated in Sagittarius or Gemini. It is possible, however, to have a square between compatible elements – such is the case when one planet is placed very near the end of a sign and another placed near the beginning of a sign, for instance, Moon at 27 degrees of Scorpio would be square Saturn at 3 degrees of Pisces. This type of square would not be quite so difficult.

THE TRINE △

Formed by planets 120 degrees apart and allowing an 8 degree orb, the trine is an aspect which allows *ease* of operation. It can give great talent or opportunities when motivated. Two usually inharmonious planets, such as Mercury and Saturn will be rendered more accessible to one another through this aspect.

Some examples of trines from our five birth charts:

Example 1 – Mars/Saturn–Moon, Pluto–Sun (note change of element here and 7 degree orb) Jupiter–Sun
Example 2 – Mars–Pluto/Venus, Saturn/Uranus–Neptune
Example 3 – Pluto–Moon
Example 4 – Pluto–Sun/Mercury
Example 5 – Sun–Saturn, Venus–Saturn

The trine is relatively easy to pick out because it usually occurs between planets situated within the same element. For example, Mars at 8 degrees of Capricorn will be trine to Pluto at 12 degrees of Virgo, and Jupiter at 1 degree of Taurus, the former utilising a 4 degree orb, the latter a 7 degree orb. However, it is possible for a trine to be formed between incompatible elements. For example, Venus at 29 degrees of Gemini would be in trine to Neptune at 4 degrees of Scorpio. These examples are harmonious, but more invigorating.

THE QUINCUNX/INCONJUNCT ⚻

The very fact that this aspect possesses two different names indicates the complexity of its workings. Planets form a quincunx when they are situated 150 degrees apart with an allowable 2–3 degree orb. The two signs involved in this aspect are nearly always of a different element and Active/Passive grouping. For example, a planet at 14 degrees of Pisces would be quincunx planets at 12 degrees Libra, and 13 degrees Leo. A planet at 2 degrees of Taurus would be quincunx planets at 1 degree of Sagittarius and 3 degrees Libra. It is regarded as a minor aspect, somewhat difficult in nature, often related to ill health, stress and adjustments in life. But like the square, when understood and utilised positively, it can give creative potential and diverse talents.

Some examples of quincunxes from our five charts:

Example 1 – None
Example 2 – Sun–Moon
Example 3 – Pluto–Saturn, Neptune/Venus–Jupiter
Example 4 – Saturn–Neptune
Example 5 – Jupiter–Pluto, Moon–Uranus, Neptune/Mars–Jupiter

The quincunx is the hardest of all the aspects for the beginner to see quickly, as there is no set grouping of elements or quadruplicities for it to fall within. Time and practice however will give you knowledge as to which signs could provide quincunxes.

THE OPPOSITION ☍

This aspect, as its name suggests involves planets which are immediately opposed to one another – that is, 180 degrees apart. Once again an orb of 8 degrees either way is allowable. The opposition is the most powerful aspect after the conjunction and square, but as it usually involves planets in signs which are compatible, such as Moon at 15 degrees of Sagittarius opposing Sun at 17 degrees of Gemini, it is rarely as problematical as the square or conjunction. One of the effects of this aspect is its see-saw motion. Subjects with this aspect prominent strive to achieve balance and eqilibrium in their lives and are therefore prone to polarities of mood.

Some examples of oppositions from the charts of our five subjects:

Example 1 – None
Example 2 – Moon–Jupiter, Mars–Neptune (this widely orbed opposition combines two different elements)
Example 3 – None
Example 4 – Saturn–Jupiter, Pluto–Moon/Mars
Example 5 – Sun–Moon, Venus–Jupiter

The opposition is easy to determine as the planets involved are opposite one another, and usually posited in complementary elements, such as fire and air, or water and earth. Watch out for the exceptions, however. Mars at 28 degrees of Taurus would still be in opposition to Pluto at 4 degrees of Sagittarius. This type of opposition could actually be more problematical, as the elements of earth and fire do not blend well.

The next step is to learn how to recognise the above aspects and place them in the aspect grid on the birth chart form.

The simplest method of finding aspects without any mechanical devices is to learn thoroughly the groupings of the signs as shown in Lesson 2 to enable you to be able to recognise instantly which type of aspect planets may be forming. One golden rule to remember is that any two planets beyond an 8 degree orb, such as Mars at 5 degrees of Aries and Jupiter at 15 degrees of Cancer *cannot* be in aspect. In this case you can instantly see the 10 degree difference signifying that Jupiter is situated precisely 100 degrees from Mars. Conversely, any planets within an 8 degree orb, such as Uranus at 19 degrees Taurus and Venus at 13 degrees Virgo (in this instance, a trine) *may* be in aspect if they can form a conjunction, square, trine or opposition and any planets with a 2 degree difference *must* form some kind of aspect, such as Moon at 18 degrees of Gemini, Mercury at 20 degrees of Capricorn (creating a quincunx).

Many beginners, however, find they cannot easily remember the groupings of the signs and prefer to count the degrees between aspects. This is perfectly acceptable and may provide more accuracy in the first instance. Simply count the degrees between the two planets (using the shortest route), always remembering to allow the appropriate degrees of orb, if necessary. Diagrams 9 and 10 demonstrate the following examples:

Diagram 9

Mars at 16 degrees Cancer is 95 degrees away from Jupiter at 21 Libra, thereby forming a square.

Neptune at 12 degrees of Scorpio is 58 degrees away from Mercury at 10 degrees of Capricorn, forming a sextile.

The Sun at 1 degree of Aquarius, is 32 degrees away from Venus at 3 degrees of Pisces, forming a semi-sextile.

The Moon at 9 degrees of Pisces is 123 degrees from Saturn at 12 degrees of Cancer, thereby forming a trine.

Diagram 10

Neptune and Saturn are in exact conjunction at 11 degrees of Sagittarius.

Jupiter at 9 degrees of Aquarius is situated 151 degrees from Venus at 10 degrees of Cancer, forming a quincunx.

Mars at 22 degrees of Aries is 175 degrees away from Pluto at 17 degrees of Libra (185 degrees apart in the opposite direction), and therefore forms an opposition.

To enter aspects on the grid simply work across from left to right starting with the Sun, comparing it with the Moon, then Mercury, then Venus, and so on, finishing with Pluto. Then work across from

DIAGRAM 9

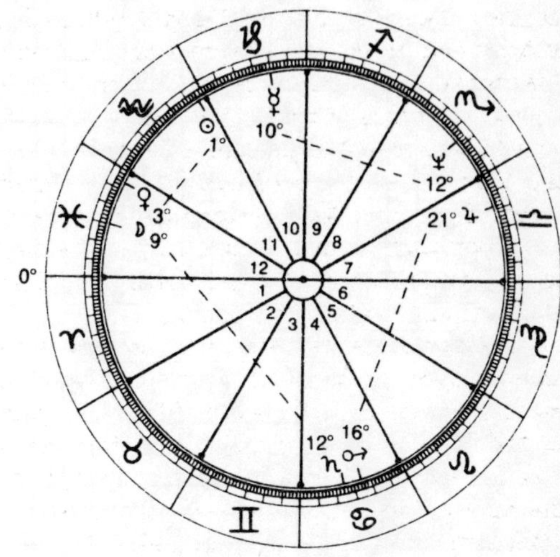

DIAGRAM 10

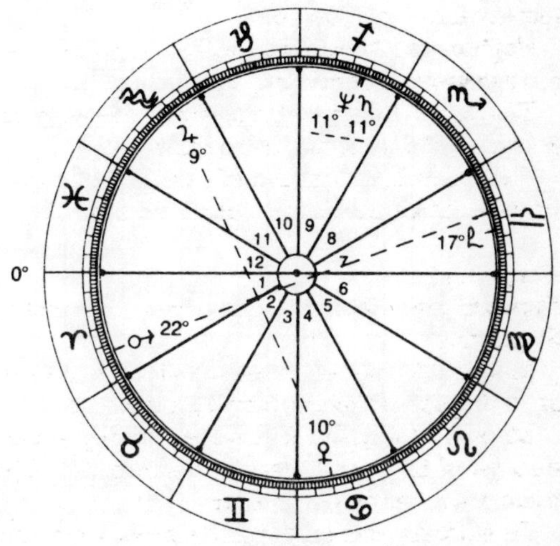

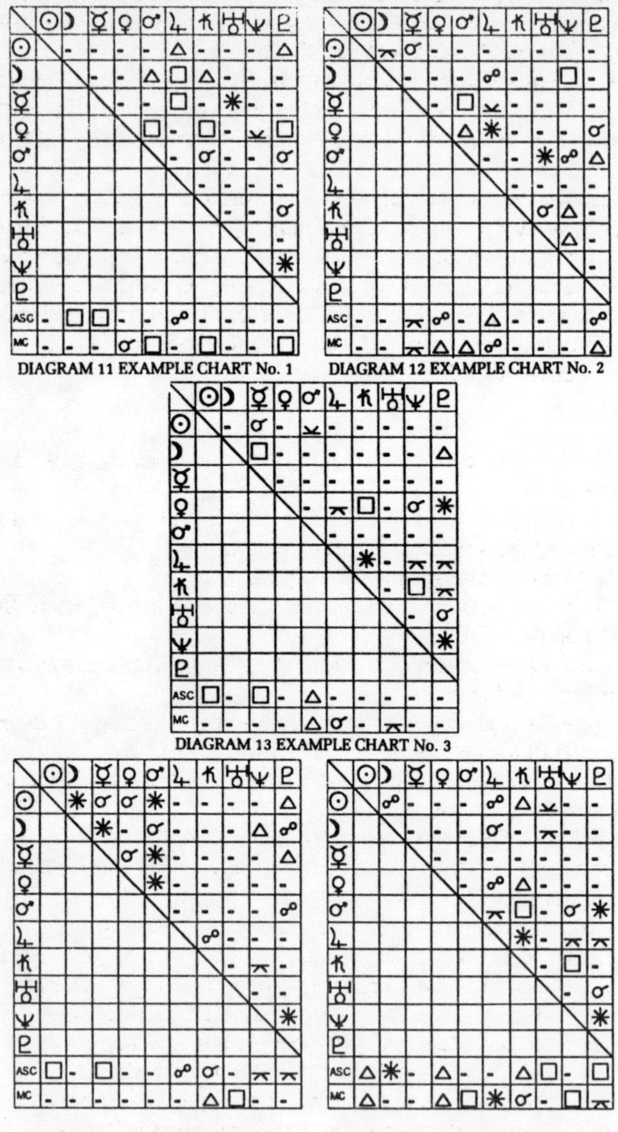

DIAGRAM 11 EXAMPLE CHART No. 1

DIAGRAM 12 EXAMPLE CHART No. 2

DIAGRAM 13 EXAMPLE CHART No. 3

DIAGRAM 14 EXAMPLE CHART No. 4

DIAGRAM 15 EXAMPLE CHART No. 5

the Moon, comparing it with Mercury, Venus, Mars, etc. Move on to Mercury, then Venus, etc, until you reach the last two planets to observe for aspects, Neptune and Pluto.

The Ascendant and Midheaven are always used when calculating aspects. Therefore work across in the same manner starting with the Ascendant to Sun, then Moon, etc. Lastly complete the Midheaven section.

If two planets make no aspect to one another it is often clearer and neater to mark the appropriate square with a dot or dash. Diagrams 11 to 15 show the aspect grids for all five of the examples used in the previous lessons. Study them carefully, ensuring that you understand the mechanics of aspect calculation, before attempting the following questionnaire. Brief interpretations of the effects of aspects in birth charts is covered in Lesson 8.

1. Which aspect is formed when two planets are exactly 90 degrees apart?
2. If Saturn were at 12 degrees of Aries, and Moon at 17 degrees of Aries which aspect would they be forming?
3. Write the symbols for all the aspects.
4. Would a planet at 10 degrees of Scorpio be aspecting another at 21 degrees of Taurus?
5. Which aspect would planets at 13 degrees of Aquarius 14 degrees of Virgo be forming?
6. Jupiter is at 29 degrees of Gemini and the Moon is at 1 degree of Leo. Is this an allowable semi-sextile?
7. What aspect would a planet at 5 degrees of Pisces be forming with another at 8 degrees of Capricorn?
8. What is the degree of orb allowed for a sextile?
9. Including the Ascendant and the Midheaven, how many conjunctions are there in Example chart No. 4?
10. Name the aspects the following would be forming:
    (a) Mars 20 degrees Sagittarius, Venus 18 degrees Pisces.
    (b) Moon 12 degrees Taurus, Saturn 15 degrees Cancer.
    (c) Jupiter 28 degrees Leo, Uranus 27 degrees Aries.
    (d) Sun 27 degrees Libra, Pluto 4 degrees Scorpio.
    (e) Moon 18 degrees Leo, Sun 20 degrees Cancer.
    (f) Neptune 2 degrees Libra, Sun 0 degrees Taurus.
    (g) Sun 29 degrees Aries, Uranus 5 degrees Scorpio.

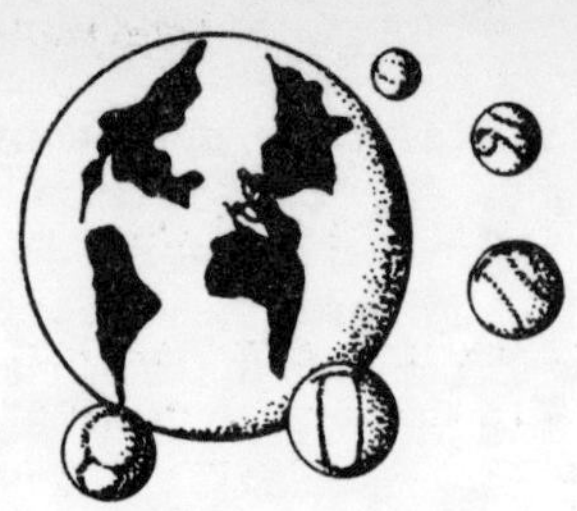

6 · INTERPRETATION: PLANETS IN SIGNS

Having completed the calculation of a birth chart it is now time to start interpreting the accumulation of symbols and facts placed before us, a complex task which cannot be achieved overnight – accurate interpretation takes time, study and patience. I would therefore recommend very strongly, to all students at this point, that they are confident in their understanding of the five preceding lessons.

In this lesson we shall be defining the significance of the ten planets when situated in the twelve signs of the zodiac. The brief interpretations are in no way conclusive, so try to add your own definitions too.

THE SUN

Rules our ego and individuality, often the deepest, innermost part of our character, which can be hidden from view. We relate to our Sun sign as being our true self, and should strive to achieve the positive characteristics of this sign in order to be living a fulfilled life. Brief keyword definitions for the position of the Sun in all twelve signs are given in Lesson 1. Go back and study these interpretations carefully and try to add your own keywords by using the characteristics of the three groupings of the signs and the energy of the ruling planet.

THE MOON

Rules our emotions, feelings, responses and habits. It is extremely important in our birth charts, often overshadowing the Sun, especially in childhood when we have not yet learnt to control our emotions. Many adults who behave irrationally, or immaturely have the Moon strongly placed in their birth chart.

Moon in Aries: An explosive, difficult placement causing sharp, irritable responses. Subject likes own way, is pushy, lacking in finesse, self-centred and childlike in attitude. Loves travelling. Possesses restless, seeking nature which exudes much fiery magetism.

Moon in Taurus: The changeable nature of the Moon is steadied in this sign, giving domesticated, practical, protective, motherly, and tenacious qualities. Subject loves land, building and structure and is fastidious with strong materialistic instincts.

Moon in Gemini: Extremely moody, restless and talkative. Fond of expressing emotions in a garrulous manner. Highly intelligent, but often unable to control feelings of duplicity, vengefulness and animosity. Exceptionally witty or overbearingly sarcastic.

Moon in Cancer: Ultra-sensitive, extremely shy and lacking in self-confidence. Strongly attached to mother or mother-figure. Seeks security and steady home-life. Cautious with finances and possessions. Dislikes letting go, possesses strong nurturing instincts.

Moon in Leo: The showman of the zodiac. Will liven up almost any birth chart with its extreme flamboyance and demonstrative reactions. Generous to a fault, loves praise and attention, but can develop tantrums and sulks if feeling unappreciated.

Moon in Virgo: Quiet, serious demeanour, exhibiting cold or unfeeling responses. Feels at ease with detailed, routine work. Health-conscious and fastidious about personal hygiene. Inner emotions chaotic and usually repressed.

Moon in Libra: Charming, likeable, attractive, intelligent and outwardly serene, these people will grace any social occasion. They can, however, be remarkably selfish, callous and unfeeling. They enjoy good conversation, harmonious surroundings and affluent company.

Moon in Scorpio: Subject experiences intense, deep feelings. Jealousy, possessiveness or anger simmer beneath a calm facade. Intuitive and probing, they make excellent psychiatrists, detectives or clairvoyants.

Mother-dominated as children, they often rebel in adulthood and find it difficult to sustain loving relationships.

Moon in Sagittarius: Changeable and moody, this configuration produces the emotional wanderer of the zodiac, lacking in concentration and loyalty. Possesses a good, but somewhat crude sense of humour. Can be impractical, buoyant, hysterical and fun-loving.

Moon in Capricorn: Repressed, inhibited emotions often caused by severe mothering are common with this placement. Subject strives for security through materialistic means and is capable of using others for his own ends. Steady and persevering, ambitious, and controlled.

Moon in Aquarius: Good, dry sense of humour. Sociable and friendly within a large group, but avoids close relationships. Independent, unusual and creatively talented, but insensitive to the feelings of others. Can, however, become deeply committed to causes, group situations, friends and social outlets.

Moon in Pisces: Dreamy, imaginative, over-sensitive, and often lacking in personal direction. Romantic, poetic, psychic, artistic and creative, they are, however, innately escapist and dislike the limelight. Changeable in affections, they can be moody, irresponsible, unreliable and prone to excesses in almost anything.

MERCURY

Rules all aspects of communication – the manner in which we learn, listen, speak, write, etc. Being so close to the Sun, it often takes on the characteristics of the Sun sign, but if placed in a different sign it operates totally independently.

Mercury in Aries: Speaks and communicates with speed, enthusiasm, boldness and confidence. Not very good at sustaining attention, or explaining anything in detail. Irritation and short-tempered verbal outbursts are common with this configuration.

Mercury in Taurus: Communication is slow, precise and laboured. Can be dull and boring in speech, but comes to life when singing (a strong Taurean talent). Enjoys communicating on a practical level, either verbally or with hands. Good business sense.

Mercury in Gemini: Situated in the sign of its rulership, Mercury is at its sparkling best. Witty, lively and irrepressible, chatty and excitable, with much surface knowledge, these people are, however, highly strung and can suffer from nervous disorders.

Mercury in Cancer: These people are invariably 'thinkers' rather than 'talkers', often finding it difficult to communicate without expressing emotion. When challenged, however, their verbal reactions can be caustic in their own defence. They possess extremely retentive memories.

Mercury in Leo: Pride, recognition and a need to be *heard*, are qualities expressed by this configuration. Sometimes, however, their propensity for 'all talk and no action' produces exaggeration, boasting or conceit, yet they can be charming, precocious and talented.

Mercury in Virgo: A good, sound mind, capable of great study and learning. Because these people absorb and pass on information quickly and efficiently, they make excellent teachers. Worry and the inability to see the other side of the situation could, however, be their downfall.

Mercury in Libra: This position produces intelligence and speed of learning. Quietly spoken with immense charm, there is always something very pleasant or polite about their demeanour. They may prefer to communicate through writing or music rather than speech.

Mercury in Scorpio: A powerful, penetrating mind. Mercury can either be extremely silent and thoughtful here, or extremely verbose. These people never forget, and rarely forgive. Their speech can be harsh, cruel or vindictive when angry, but gentle and soothing when in a caring situation.

Mercury in Sagittarius: Extremely communicative, restless and volatile, with a pressing need to talk about anything and everything. These people often give the impression of being more knowledgeable than they really are, and can outwit anybody. They have a hearty sense of humour and love to play pranks or jokes.

Mercury in Capricorn: Quiet, serious manner of expression which may seem taciturn or uncaring. These people find it extremely difficult to communicate, and are often very slow learners. When knowledge is absorbed, however, it is never forgotten, and always put to practical, sound use.

Mercury in Aquarius: Produces inventive, ingenious minds, with unusual or erratic manner of communicating. They learn quickly and retain information, but often appear supercilious, and difficult to approach. They are greatly attracted to modern technology as means of communication.

Mercury in Pisces: Tends to communicate on a vague, dreamy level. Brilliant imagination and creative ability, but often unable to structure their capabilities. Will either chat incessantly or remain agonisingly shy and quiet – depending upon whom they are with. These people lack concentration yet are able to absorb knowledge like a sponge.

VENUS

This planet represents love and harmony. It reveals what, who and how we love, and also our values in life. It is *not* the 'gut' feeling represented by the Moon, but more our mode of appreciation and enjoyment.

Venus in Aries: These people love ardently and fiercely. Quick to show appreciation and quick to tire, they need constant stimulation. They enjoy excitement and danger, and love being in the limelight. They may find it difficult to be loyal or faithful when their sense of adventure is roused.

Venus in Taurus: Placed in a sign of its rulership, Venus is very much at home and can therefore be lazy, complacent and even-tempered. Musical or singing talent is common. These people usually feel in tune with the beauty of nature and like to be in close contact with the land.

Venus in Gemini: Flirtatious, light-hearted and inoffensive, those with Venus in this sign are usually popular, but they can be deceitful or untruthful when confronted with difficult situations. Inconstant, yet delightfully naive, they are easily forgiven. They enjoy talking and communicating on a convivial level.

Venus in Cancer: This sign tends to bring out the best in Venus. These people love with sensitivity, tenderness and compassion. They enjoy entertaining at home, raising a family, photography, films and dealing with antiques. Conscious of the material world, but capable of great acts of charity.

Venus in Leo: Adulation, luxury and adornment, are vitally desired by these subjects in order that they may project their loving, generous and loyal qualities. If deprived of these requisites they wilt and become sullen and ego-centred. Theatrical involvement is one way in which they can command the respect they crave.

Venus in Virgo: Renowned for their purity and analytical detachment, these complex people often feel misunderstood or underrated. They are extremely fussy, and critical, yet adore animals, small pets especially, whom they turn to for the affection often lacking in their lives.

Venus in Libra: This configuration adds charm, pleasantness and refinement to even the most difficult of birth charts. It can, however, also be conducive to narcissism. Music, dance, art or drama appeals strongly to their aesthetic natures. They believe in justice and harmony, but are rarely very demonstrative when in love.

Venus in Scorpio: Loves deeply, with either much possessiveness, jealousy and insecurity, or with passion, generosity and kindness. They are capable, however, of controlling their feelings of love and withdrawing from society completely. They appreciate mystery, seductiveness, allure, and uninhibited sexuality.

Venus in Sagittarius: Amorous and well-intentioned this person seeks freedom *and* security in a relationship, a regular once-a-week tryst being regarded as idyllic. They possess a good sense of humour and appreciation of anything large, including animals such as horses, and enjoy active sports.

Venus in Capricorn: Usually quiet, with an appreciation of serious matters, this person is often labelled prudish or frigid, which is far from the truth – they just take longer than most people to warm up. Capable of extreme frugality, they shun luxury and adornment, especially in their youth. They tend to look and act younger than their years.

Venus in Aquarius: Charming and sociable, yet detached and unsympathetic, these subjects enjoy projecting themselves. They are attracted to scientific or electronic gadgets and anything to do with aviation. Often labelled as unfeeling and cold, they will avoid any demonstrations of affection.

Venus in Pisces: Altruistic, soft and loving, yet careless and disorganised, this position produces both saints and sinners. Romantic, sensitive and artistic, they yearn for love and harmony, which all too often alludes them, causing them to become prey to such vices as escapism, decadence or addiction. Self-sacrifice is common.

MARS

Physical energy, assertiveness, aggression, sexual and sporting activity and violence all fall under the domain of this highly masculine planet. It toughens and dominates the area of the birth chart in which it is found.

Mars in Aries: Placed within the sign that it rules Mars is in its prime, endowing its subjects with unlimited energy, a tremendous sense of adventure and a desire to live life to the full, but used negatively it can produce anger, violence, bullying and aggressiveness. These people should *always* lead a physically active life to allow their pent-up energy full rein.

Mars in Taurus: Physically strong and remarkably enduring. Even if not in a prominent position will add girth and solidity to the subject's frame. Usually attracted to the earth and nature-orientated sports such as rambling, rock-climbing or mountaineering, or to sports involving stamina, such as rugby or boxing. Highly sensual, but rigid and stubborn and can be cruel when the energy is used negatively.

Mars in Gemini: Hyperactivity, neuroticism and lack of physical stamina are common with this placement. Intelligent and talkative, however, they crave constant communication – in fact it may be difficult for anybody else to get a word in edgeways. They are attracted to mind games such as chess or bridge, and any occupations involving swift, skilful reactions. They prefer to talk about their physical needs rather than act them out.

Mars in Cancer: Regarded as a difficult position for this fiery planet, the energy being swamped with emotionalism, sensitivity and over-protectiveness. Their nurturing instincts can be too strong at times, but their sexually magnetic natures assure that they will never be short of amorous advances. Water sports, especially swimming or scuba-diving, will attract them.

Mars in Leo: The dare-devil exhibitionists of the zodiac, whose egos inspire them to reach the top in whatever they attempt. They are attracted to anything involving speed and excitement, such as car or speed-boat racing, but in common with their namesake, the Lion, they also possess a surprisingly lazy streak and enjoy basking in the sun. As with all the fixed signs, this position of Mars can lead to cruelty, aggression or violence if not channelled properly.

Mars in Virgo: The assertive energy of Mars finds it difficult to prosper in this small-thinking sign – a situation which leads to much carping or criticism, and over-concern with health, hygiene or diet on the part of the subject. A good position, however, for the healing profession, both orthodox and alternative. Fast, earthy sports, such as football, tennis, cricket will appeal, but the incentive to exert physical energy is often lacking.

Mars in Libra: The competitive energy of Mars is somewhat depleted in this sign, more preference being shown for mental or creative endeavours, although air sports such as hang-gliding, parachuting or aeroplane-flying will strongly appeal. Usually inoffensive and charming, these people are well-liked, but possess the strange knack of attracting the qualities they dislike most – disharmony and aggression, possibly caused by their extreme indecisiveness and love of justice.

Mars in Scorpio: Extremely powerful, yet one of the most difficult positions for Mars. The deep intense level of their desires and emotions, renders it difficult for these people to remain composed. Feelings of hate, jealousy, aggression or vindictiveness are therefore easily aroused. These subjects make marvellous, loyal friends, but vengeful enemies. They are highly sexed, determined and excelling in sporting activity.

Mars in Sagittarius: Situated here, the abundant energy of Mars instils its subjects with extreme restlessness. These people will talk with great enthusiasm about anything, impress others with their marvellous physical skills – athletics, archery and horse-riding are amongst their favourites – and keep you laughing with their tremendous sense of humour, but they can be remarkably thick-skinned and insensitive to the feelings of others. Constancy and loyalty are not very high on their list of priorities.

Mars in Capricorn: Mars is exalted in this sign (Lesson 8 explains this term), enabling the energy to be used practically, cautiously and methodically, but the hardness of this configuration renders it difficult for the subject to use sensitivity and balance in his judgement. He can be officious, ambitious, hardworking, calculating, sensual and sly with good business or financial acumen. Slow sports requiring high concentration, such as bowls or snooker, appeal, as do earthy activities such as mountaineering.

Mars in Aquarius: Independent, intelligent, strong-willed and highly individualistic, this position of Mars endows its subjects with an abundance of mental energy with which to pursue a great variety of creative outlets. These subjects are undeniably loyal, friendly and likeable providing they get their own way, but they can be verbally abusive or extremely haughty if thwarted in their aims. Air sports, and games involving speed and skill appeal greatly, and for an air sign they possess surprising physical prowess.

Mars in Pisces: This is a difficult position for Mars, because much of the energy is emotionally diffused. In this sign Mars can become a leech, using martyrdom, guilt and passion as its tools. Direction in life is often difficult thereby resulting in addiction, alcoholism or immoral attitudes. On a more positive level, Mars in Pisces can produce compassion and saintly deeds. Psychic abilities are strong and should be controlled. Water sports and football appeal.

JUPITER

With Jupiter, the largest and most gaseous planet in our solar system, we begin to veer away from the personalisation of the first five planets. Jupiter rules our desire to expand, be it mentally or physically, and is usually regarded as a positive influence. It can, however, open up and make worse any difficulties arising in the birth chart and is therefore not always the great benefic it is renowned to be. Take this into account when reading the interpretations below.

Jupiter in Aries: Expands the need for domination, excitement, adventure, conquest and physical needs. Adds extrovertism, brashness, impulsiveness and speed to the character. Self-centred, innovative and basically lucky.

Jupiter in Taurus: Adds solidity, materialism, earthiness, stability, musical ability, and an innate love of the earth. Dependable, financially secure, and sensual, fire-ruled Jupiter is strangely at ease in this heavy earth sign.

Jupiter in Gemini: The expansive qualities of Jupiter are difficult to control in this light air sign. Too much knowledge can be accumulated in a chaotic fashion, causing communication problems. Intelligent, highly verbose and multi-talented.

Jupiter in Cancer: Usually kind, sensitive and compassionate, these people possess excellent nurturing instincts and good financial prowess, but can be over-possessive, highly emotional and too concerned with home affairs. Weight may be a problem.

Jupiter in Leo: This configuration usually commands great respect and is considered very fortunate. Loyal, dignified and honest, these people possess a tremendous capacity to give, but sometimes their love of luxury, adornment and riches undermines their innate generosity. Theatrical, magnetic and physically strong,

Jupiter in Virgo: Jupiter finds it difficult to blossom within this sign. Expansion is limited, fussy and detailed. Projects are logical and commendable, but rarely able to succeed due to lack of grandeur, and the necessary implementation. Good practical ability, however.

Jupiter in Libra: Finesse, good judgement, charm and success are to be found with this placement. Justice, law and order will attract, as will music, art and drama. Considered a beneficial position for Jupiter, but excessive weight gain and prevarication are two problems which may arise.

Jupiter in Scorpio: Intense and dedicated, passionate and probing, Jupiter here does not like to leave anything untouched once the interest has been aroused. Good financial judgement and keen absorption of knowledge and human nature. Can, however, be over-sexed, possessive and aggressive if the emotions are allowed too much sway.

Jupiter in Sagittarius: In the sign that it rules, Jupiter revels in its freedom and cognition of the world. Optimism, faith, humour, love of variety and learning are all strongly featured within this individual. Sometimes, though, they can go overboard with their enthusiasm to the cost of everything else and lose much of what they value or cherish.

Jupiter in Capricorn: A hard, unpretentious worker, with good sound practical sense. Ambitious and determined, yet able to wait for the right moment to advance, Jupiter positioned here can do much to open up the normally reserved Capricorn character.

Jupiter in Aquarius: A love of freedom combined with great mental activity. These subjects are friendly and outgoing, with a projection of warmth normally lacking in the detached Aquarian. Eccentric, individualistic manner, incorporating much talent and ability. Dedication to causes and group activities.

Jupiter in Pisces: The old ruler of Pisces is still very much in tune with this sign and tends to bring out its best qualities – sensitivity, compassion, creativity, imagination, healing ability, saintliness, religious interests, etc., thereby making its subjects more able to cope with the realities of life.

SATURN

Totally opposite in its characteristics to Jupiter, Saturn is supposedly restrictive, fearsome and cold, but it is also life's greatest teacher. We all have to learn, and if we accept the wisdom and discipline of Saturn its energy becomes positive and beneficial, rather than frustrating and depressive.

Saturn in Aries: Not an easy position for Saturn – Aries likes action but Saturn demands caution. The subject desires prominence, freedom and self-assertiveness, often becoming aggressive when seeking his own path, but Saturn here is warning of a need for more patience, and less impulsiveness. All too often these people will act first, then think and regret later. They see themselves as victimised and burdened by responsibilities, and unable to progress in life. When they learn to control their own selfish urges they will automatically become respected.

Saturn in Taurus: Saturn copes well here – both sign and planet are slow in movement and serious in nature. The subject may, however, feel inferior, dull, and lifeless when compared with brighter individuals, and find it difficult to be light-hearted or optimistic, often placing too much value on financial security. Some of these subjects work hard all their lives with seemingly little reward but others become victims of the Taurean laziness and lead very stagnant lives. They need to learn to accept themselves as practical, useful and hardworking members of the community, whereupon their material needs will become less important.

Saturn in Gemini: The restrictions, fears and frustrations experienced by these people are usually all in the mind. They imagine they cannot communicate, or talk as freely as they wish, but in reality they are the opposite, often burdening others with their pessimistic outlook and loquacious tongue. Mental and psychosomatic problems therefore frequently occur. When Saturn in Gemini gains confidence, stops looking on the bleak side and comes to terms with its own unique brand of communication, either by conversing, writing or teaching, the doubts and depression fade into the distance forever.

Saturn in Cancer: This position of Saturn bestows its subjects with excellent nurturing abilities, making them marvellous parents and home-makers. In youth, however, they often deny these needs, appearing to be hard, insensitive and calculating. They may fear the responsibilities of a home and family and seek solace within their own inner world. When they finally accept themselves as normal human beings with strong, sensitive emotions and caring instincts, they become pillars of society. If they marry and endeavour to raise a family before accepting themselves, it will be inducive to a very difficult home environment.

Saturn in Leo: The fun-loving, flamboyant characteristics of Leo are deeply ingrained within this individual, but rarely able to flow freely. The serious, heavy nature of Saturn overshadows the Leo exhibitionism, especially during youth, causing these people to project themselves quietly when they would prefer to be thrust into the limelight. They often fear ridicule and rejection so much that they will remain in the background until they are totally confident of their reception. When they learn that it is far more rewarding to be spontaneous they quickly become aware of the captivated, adulating audience which awaits them.

Saturn in Virgo: This configuation can work quite well. Both planet and sign love detail and conscientious, practical work. Saturn here is capable of great learning, but the extreme introversion of this combination incites intimidation, insecurity and fearfulness. Strong depression and pessimism can also occur, and although over-critical themselves the slightest amount of criticism from others easily dissuades them from using their tremendous potential. When they come to terms with the fact that although they are basically shy, logical and practical, they are in no way inferior to anybody else, and can excel in anything they attempt.

Saturn in Libra: Regarded as one of the better positions for Saturn, being in exaltation (see Lesson 8), but in reality this is not always the case. The positive qualities of Libra – charm, diplomacy, harmony, justness and finesse – are often hidden when Saturn falls here. The subject fears being too nice, and will purposefully repress his pleasant characteristics, often being rude or dogmatic in the process. When he finally learns that nobody is going to take advantage of him or defile his talents when he endeavours to be pleasant, affable and charming, he will command respect, being much sought after for his knowledge and advice.

Saturn in Scorpio: The person with Saturn here is terrified of showing his feelings. Emotions are continuously denied, even though his heart craves an outlet. He may also deny his powerful sexuality and feelings of jealousy or resentment, eventually resulting in a torrent of pent-up feelings being expelled in a very aggressive manner. This person is sensitive to *everything* around him but he may appear cold, ruthless, and utterly heartless until he learns to let go of his emotions in a loving, sensitive manner. If he can do so – which is a tall order, because no other sign finds it quite so difficult to adapt and change as Scorpio – he will be loved and cherished throughout his life.

Saturn in Sagittarius: The Sagittarian urge for freedom and change is hindered with Saturn here. The subject feels unable to allow the adventurous, resourceful side of his nature full rein. He limits his natural optimism and lively temperament and can become melancholic or depressive. He fears showing enthusiasm and will suppress his natural desire to learn and acquire knowledge by demeaning himself. As always, with Saturn, maturity (which can arrive at any age) is the key to the unlocking of the door. When Saturn in Sagittarius decides to open up, speak and say the truth, express his urge to travel and learn, and realise his capabilities, he will go far both mentally and physically.

Saturn in Capricorn: Placed within the sign that it rules Saturn works well, although it does endow its subjects with a serious nature and strong materialistic ideals. These people can also become too enmeshed in the practical side of life, being unable to see the wood for the trees. Single-minded dedication, determination, loyalty and steadiness are all good qualities when used openly without fear, but too often the subject will use these qualities solely for his own use, until such time when they are no longer needed, then discard them from his life quite ruthlessly. The lesson here for these people is to learn to give themselves and their capabilities simply and honestly, without using others or desiring something in return.

Saturn in Aquarius: The old ruler of this sign tends to bring out the more serious contemplative characteristics of the sign, the innate desire for independence and excitement being quelled. The subjects will conform but in a resentful manner, feeling restricted by imagined burdens and responsibilities. Sometimes they project an unfriendly image – they *want* to be amicable and sociable but find it difficult to be so. Most of the feelings of limitation are on a mental level because although they are extremely intelligent and able to absorb knowledge well, they can be slow in doing so, and imagine themselves lacking in this respect. They need to learn that in order to be readily accepted as responsible citizens, it is not essential to attain knowledge quickly, or to worry about their dispassionate image.

Saturn in Pisces: The emotions do not flow easily with this configuration. Pisces needs to eliminate its worries, fears and negativity through tears and open displays of emotion and affection, but Saturn here blocks this urge, regarding these responses as immature, and demands sensibility. This combination, therefore, can produce a young person with a very old head upon his shoulders, desperately seeking to be recognised as learned and wise, but not being successful in achieving this status because he has not experienced the traumas of life in the manner demanded by the sign of Pisces. To Saturn's credit here, however, the common Piscean traits of addiction, disorientation and immorality are far less likely to occur.

URANUS, NEPTUNE AND PLUTO

These three planets take a long time to transit one sign and are regarded as generational. In interpreting the birth chart, therefore, their sign position is less significant than their house position. Very briefly, however, they can be interpreted within the signs, as follows:

Uranus in Aries: Galvanising, exciting, magnetic, highly abrasive, impulsive, and self-centred.

Uranus in Taurus: De-structuralising, uniquely talented, unusual singing voice, strong-tempered.

Uranus in Gemini: Extremely excitable, intelligent, mentally alert, moody, hyperactive.

Uranus in Cancer: Disruptive home and family life, gifted children, detached emotions, sulky and wilful.

Uranus in Leo: Magnanimous, eccentric, highly effusive, rebellious, remarkable achievements.

Uranus in Virgo: Difficulty in controlling mental and practical outlets. Overloaded mental system. Neurotic.

Uranus in Libra: Unique charm, distant and cold, flair for design and form sudden change of opinion.

Uranus in Scorpio: Dynamic, cruel or vindictive, unusual sexual responses, natural leader, hypnotic physical appeal.

Uranus in Sagittarius: An explorer, highly intelligent bordering upon genius, crazy, insensitive, self-absorbed.

Uranus in Capricorn: Far-seeing, highly ambitious, cold, ruthless, mechanically or practically talented.

Uranus in Aquarius: Inventive, scientific, space-age, eccentric, rebellious, non-conformist.

Uranus in Pisces: Highly gifted, powerful imagination, disruptive emotions, moody, unreliable, mentally unstable.

Neptune in Aries: Dominant leadership qualities used in a hypnotic manner. Disorientation whilst travelling. Head illnesses or disorders.

Neptune in Taurus: Artistic, musical, beautiful, living in a fantasy world, a financial disaster.

Neptune in Gemini: Unstable, visionary, head in the clouds, erratic, changeable, gifted.

Neptune in Cancer: Extremely psychic or intuitive water-loving, confused home-life, ultra-sensitive.

Neptune in Leo: Tremendous acting potential, generous, charitable, artitistic, magnetic, unstable.

Neptune in Virgo: Becomes confused over small details, untidy, mentally brilliant but chaotic mind, lacks vision.

Neptune in Libra: Love of harmony, beauty and peace, creative or artistic, extremely indecisive, easily swayed, searching for ideal love.

Neptune in Scorpio: Deep, confused emotions, lack of control, potential for vice or addiction, extremely psychic, imaginative and erotic.

Neptune in Sagittarius: Enthusiasm diffused, a loner or wanderer, unsettled mentally and physically, amorous.

Neptune in Capricorn: Visionary and artistic in a practical manner. Lack of structure in life, highly sensual, disorganised.

Neptune in Aquarius: Vague, dreamlike, evasive, devotion to human rights, mentally unstable.

Neptune in Pisces: Great empathy, compassion and sensitivity, a dreamer, saintly, sacrificial, magnetic, not of this world or unable to cope with life's realities.

Pluto in Aries: Volcanic, aggressive, a born leader, heated passion, love of power and control.

Pluto in Taurus: Strong will-power, violent temper, intense love of the land, utterly reliable.

Pluto in Gemini: Powerful manner of speech or communication, volatile, sadistic, highly intelligent.

Pluto in Cancer: Over-protective, possessive and jealous. Deep-rooted emotions. Trauma in early family life.

Pluto in Leo: Obsessive desire to be noticed, magnetic leadership qualities, strong-willed, controlling.

Pluto in Virgo: Obsessive about hygiene. Powerful sex-drive, capable of great detail, worries about minor details of life.

Pluto in Libra: Charming in a powerful, hypnotic manner, thrives on admiration, aggressive in pursuit of justice.

Pluto in Scorpio: Intense feelings of every kind, violent temper, uneasy childhood, destructive, wilful, psychic, marvellous memory.

Pluto in Sagittarius: Tremendous urge to travel, intense about learning, prophetic, powerful leader, quick-tempered.

Pluto in Capricorn: Strong sense of duty and responsibility, feelings of being overburdened. Sensual and manipulating.

Pluto in Aquarius: Highly individualistic, intense about scientific, computerised age, unfeeling, dominant.

Pluto in Pisces: Emotions experienced with deep intensity, prone to the very worst in addiction, self-destructive, powerful healer, great extremist.

Take great care with the following questions, and attempt to answer without reference to the text, using as many words as possible. Only move on to the next lesson when you are satisfied that you can give at least one satisfactory keyword for each of the above interpretations.

1. Describe a person with Venus in Pisces.
2. Would somebody with Mars in Libra be physically energetic?
3. How does Saturn affect the sign of Cancer?
4. What does the Sun represent within a birth chart?
5. Describe the characteristics of Jupiter in Leo.
6. If a person were keen on water sports which sign(s) might you expect Mars to be placed in?
7. Describe the function of the Moon in a birth chart.
8. Where might Mercury be placed if a person spoke slowly, cautiously and sensibly?
9. Are the three outer planets more important within the signs or houses of the birth chart?
10. What effect does Saturn have upon our lives?

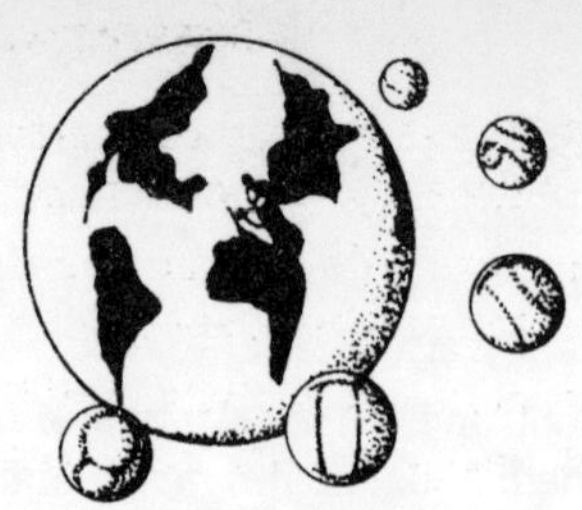

7 · Interpretation: Planets in Houses

It is now time to move on to the most fascinating, yet often the most neglected part of astrological interpretation – *the houses*. There are many different methods of house division but the system used within this book – the Equal House system, which contains twelve equally proportioned houses of 30 degrees, as represented in our diagrams in Lesson 5 – is the most ancient, simple and balanced method of all.

The houses can be divided into three groups as follows:

Angular – 1st, 4th, 7th and 10th.
Succedent – 2nd, 5th, 8th and 11th.
Cadent – 3rd, 6th, 9th and 12th.

Planets situated in the angular houses appear to have more impact upon the birth chart and are therefore regarded as being very important, especially when placed within an 8 degree orb of the relevant house cusp. Generally speaking planets in angular houses initiate situations which are then implemented by the planets in succedent houses, to be finally improved or modified by the planets in cadent houses.

Each house is representative of a certain *area* of life, and a planet situated within a house will automatically render this 'area' of great importance.

Ascendant/First House: The sign on the cusp (beginning) of the first house is always the Ascendant (Rising Sign), and as such is the main indicator of the outer personality, the appearance and the immediate impact projection of the subject upon others.

Second house: Financial and monetary concerns, earning potential, possessions, values, lower senses, appetite.

Third house: Daily mundane activity, childhood education, short-distance travel, all relatives other than parents, writing, teaching, general communication.

Fourth house: One of the parents, usually the father. Home and private life, hereditary factors, inner emotions.

Fifth house: Creativity, children, sports, hobbies, romantic attachments, gambling, social instinct.

Sixth house: Work environment, service given and received, health interests, small animals or pets.

Seventh house: Relationships – marital or business, childhood friendships, open enemies or conflict.

Eighth house: Birth, death, inheritance, partner's monetary concerns, sexuality, psychic and spiritual interests.

Ninth house: Long-distance travel, higher learning, religion, philosophy, teaching.

Tenth house: Aims, ambitions and fulfilment. One of the parents, usually the mother.

Eleventh house: Friends, groups and societies, social activity.

Twelfth house: Hospitals, prisons, charities, large institutions, guilts, secrets, sorrows, self-destruction, religious and spiritual concerns.

When analysing the planets in the houses we are interpreting the *area* of life in which the planet requires expression. The following gives a brief example of how the ten planets might be expressed in each house.

SUN

First: The ego and individuality are directed towards the self, giving a strong personality with much egotism, self-centredness and pride.

Second: The ego and individuality are directed towards finances, possessions and values. Good earning potential and business ability.

Third: The ego and individuality are directed towards communication of all kinds. A restless nature with a need for learning, commitment to relatives and daily activity.

Fourth: The ego and individuality are directed towards the home. Father will figure strongly in the life. A need for privacy and domestic attachments.

Fifth: The ego and individuality are directed towards creative expression. Children and romantic attachments provide much gratification.

Sixth: The ego and individuality are directed towards work. Beneficial or detrimental to health depending upon aspects. Good rapport with animals.

Seventh: The ego and individuality are directed towards partnerships of all kinds, and can only be expressed clearly when involved with another person.

Eighth: The ego and individuality are directed towards anything related to or given by other people. Absorbs and holds in emotions for the purpose of ego gratification. Strong passions.

Ninth: The ego and individuality are directed towards higher learning and study and a need for reaching out towards others. Travelling satisfies these urges, as does religious study.

Tenth: The ego and individuality are directed towards ambitions and fulfilment. Needs to be successful in endeavours or prominent within chosen career.

Eleventh: The ego and individuality are directed towards maintaining support from friendships and group activities.

Twelfth: The ego and individuality are directed towards secretivity, hospitals and institutions. Self-denial, frustrated self-expression or destructive tendencies may be present.

Note: The Sun is regarded as a masculine energy and therefore represents anything masculine within our lives – fathers, brothers, uncles, etc. Sun in the third house, for instance, would depict male relatives, Sun in the sixth, male co-workers, Sun in the eleventh male friends. It can also indicate traditionally male-orientated practices, such as maintaining and supporting, assertion, discipline, respect and physically dominated sports.

MOON

First: The emotions, habits and responses are expressed openly, via the personality. Physically, the features will either be plump, pale, weak and rounded, or thin, dark, sallow and sharp.

greatly by lively mother.

Eleventh: The urge to communicate is focused upon friends and group activities. Lively, versatile and chatty with friends. Enjoys group discussion.

Twelfth: The urge to communicate is repressed and submerged into the imagination, which can then become over active. Mental illness occurs if not used positively. Secretive, delving mind with many unused talents.

Note: Mercury is regarded as being sexless, and is therefore neutral in its qualities. It is more at ease in the cadent houses, where it produces creative, imaginative minds, but is also more prone to mental instability and nervousness.

VENUS

First: The desire for love, peace and harmony is conveyed by a charming, pleasant personality. Attractive appearance, but the subject often values himself too highly.

Second: The desire for love, peace and harmony is channelled through materialistic and sensual needs, or through a great love of nature.

Third: The desire for love, peace and harmony is expressed through conversation, writing or artistic endeavours. Good rapport with relatives, siblings and teachers.

Fourth: The desire for love, peace and harmony is exhibited within the home environment. Values home and contents highly. Loving father.

Fifth: The desire for love, peace and harmony is asserted spontaneously through creative endeavours, through a love of children, and with a need for romantic liaisons and much social activity.

Sixth: The desire for love, peace and harmony is channelled into maintaining a pleasant working environment and an appreciation of health interests. Love of animals.

Seventh: The desire for love, peace and harmony is extremely strong within relationships. Enjoys giving or receiving love. Attracts good influences from others.

Eighth: The desire for love, peace and harmony is expressed mainly through the physical needs of a relationship. Inheritance, and acquisition of possessions are indicated. Loves deeply.

Ninth: The desire for love, peace and harmony is projected outwardly into study, religion, philosophy, etc. Love of travelling and foreign subjects.

Tenth: The desire for love, peace and harmony is expressed through the career. Drawn to artistic, feminine careers such as fashion, hairdressing or beauty consultancy. Attractive, charming mother.

Eleventh: The desire for love, peace and harmony is channelled into friendships and beneficial group activities. Charming, artistic friends with strong materialistic instincts.

Twelfth: The desire for love, peace and harmony is depicted by a need for solitude and meditation. Appreciates hospitals and institutions. May even be happy living a restricted, secluded life.

Note: Venus is very much a feminine planet and produces feminine influences within the house it occupies. A man with Venus in the tenth, for example, will still be attracted to feminine-orientated careers. It produces a desire to be pleasant and harmonious in whatever area of life it is represented, but it can also emit laziness, sensuality and love of materialism.

MARS

First: Energy, drive and enthusiasm radiate from the personality. Aggressiveness may also be apparent. The features will be strong, signifying power and authority.

Second: Energy, drive and enthusiasm are directed into material issues. Excellent earning potential and accumulation of possessions. Overbearing attitudes.

Third: Energy, drive and enthusiasm are channelled into communication. Powerful speaker or writer. Dominance meted out or received from relatives.

Fourth: Energy, drive and enthusiasm are focused upon home affairs. Assertive and dominant in private matters. Powerful, aggressive father and/or difficult upbringing.

Fifth: Energy, drive and enthusiasm are ignited by romantic attachments, children and creative pursuits. Dominant towards children. Sportingly active.

Sixth: Energy, drive and enthusiasm are channelled into work – workaholics often possess this position of Mars, with resulting health problems. Dominant or aggressive with animals.

Seventh: Energy, drive and enthusiasm are directed into relationships. Will dominate or be dominated by partner. Arguments occur frequently.

Eighth: Energy, drive and enthusiasm are greatly controlled, but tremendously powerful. Strong sexual urges and an innate ability to accumulate anything from others.

Ninth: Energy, drive and enthusiasm are expelled through learning and travelling. Assertiveness and influential ability is strong. Could be a religious leader.

Tenth: Energy, drive and enthusiasm are directed into ambition and career. The Army, Police Force or any highly physical, male-dominated occupation would appeal. Powerful mother.

Eleventh: Energy, drive and enthusiasm are sustained by powerful friendships. Attracts, or strongly reacts to, assertive, aggressive people or group situations.

Twelfth: Energy, drive and enthusiasm are hidden and difficult to release. Secret physical or sexual prowess. Self-destructive tendencies and great interest in hospital or institution activities.
Note: Mars is a strongly masculine planet and gives energy, strength and assertiveness to the area in which it falls. It can also add aggression, violence or selfishness. The house which Mars occupies is the area of life in which we like to rule or be number one. Mars does not give in easily, much preferring war to harmony, and action to passivity.

JUPITER

First: Expansiveness and optimism are expressed openly in the personality. Height or girth is added to the frame, especially in later years. Likeable person.

Second: Expansiveness and optimism are used in material concerns. Good fortune and earning potential. Tendency to overeat and revel in the luxuries of life.

Third: Expansiveness and optimism are directed towards others. Much beneficial short-distance travel and encouragement from relatives. Thinks and acts 'big'.

Fourth: Expansiveness and optimism are discharged within the home. Appreciative of spacious, rambling premises. Beneficial father or genial upbringing.

Fifth: Expansiveness and optimism are shown towards children and romantic attachments, which may be many in number. Lucky gambling instincts. Enjoys social activities.

Sixth: Expansiveness and optimism manifest within working conditions. Likeable working companions. Good health and recuperative powers. Love of large animals.

Seventh: Expansiveness and optimism are projected into partnerships. Elevated or influential partner. General benefits through business or marital relationships.

Eighth: Expansiveness and optimism are directed towards other people's resources. Inheritance and accumulation of possessions likely. Good investigatory powers.

Ninth: Expansiveness and optimism are generated by travel and learning. Religion and philosophy are widely studied. Adds wisdom and positivity to the chart.

Tenth: Expansiveness and optimism are generated through the career. A position of authority, power and respect is desired. Politics, the stock market, acting or teaching should appeal.

Eleventh: Expansiveness and optimism are bestowed upon, and received from, friends. Positions of authority within group situations are accorded. Luck through influential friends.

Twelfth: Expansiveness and optimism are witheld from daily activities. Tremendous imagination and capacity for secret life. Hospital, charitable and religious work beneficial.
Note: Jupiter is predominantly masculine and far-reaching in its effects, being regarded as highly fortunate within the area it occupies. It can, however, generate too much of a good thing. For example, in the first house it can enlarge the physical frame to enormous proportions, in the second house it can cause extravagance and in the tenth too much ambition, etc.

SATURN

First: Limitation seriousness, fears and lack of confidence are projected into the personality. There is often restriction on weight or growth and/or sallow features.

Second: Limitation, seriousness, fears and lack of confidence are experienced with material concerns, which often leads to parsimony. Restrictions on possessions and appetite. Rigid values.

Third: Limitation, seriousness, fears and lack of confidence are projected through communication, relatives and daily activity. Learning problems and fears regarding transport. Often 'only' or 'lonely' children.

Fourth: Limitation, seriousness, fears and lack of confidence are expressed in the home. Extreme difficulty in showing feelings. Severe, disciplinary or unloving father or lonely upbringing. Good, responsible home-maker.

Fifth: Limitation, seriousness, fears and lack of confidence are revealed in creative endeavours and sporting activities. Harsh with children. Slow to form romantic attachments.

Sixth: Limitation, seriousness, fears and lack of confidence are experienced in work situations. Weak constitution. Either workaholic or afraid of work. May be frightened of animals.

Seventh: Limitation, seriousness, fears and lack of confidence are encountered in relationships. Attraction to older partners – possibly seeking parental substitute. Delays and frustrations within marriage.

Eighth: Limitation, seriousness, fears and lack of confidence are suffered within physical relationships. Partners' resources minimal or inadequate. Delays in inheritance. Birth problems in females.

Ninth: Limitation, seriousness, fears and lack of confidence are keenly felt when studying or learning. Travel arrangements thwarted or delayed. Serious and dedicated about religion and principles.

Tenth: Limitation, seriousness, fears and lack of confidence are sustained through the career. Strong ambition but delays in achieving success and fulfilment. Desirous of positions of authority and responsibility.

Eleventh: Limitation, seriousness, fears and lack of confidence are experienced in group situations. Finds it difficult to relate closely to friends, but loyal and responsible towards them.

Twelfth: Limitation, seriousness, fears and lack of confidence are deeply ingrained but rarely expressed openly. Often feels obligated or responsible for the actions of others. Depression is common.

Note: Saturn is basically feminine and passive in its energy. The area of life in which it falls is often beset with difficulties and frustrations, especially before middle age, but it also teaches us lessons in life and can eventually become quite fortunate in its effects. For example, a person with Saturn in the second may, after years of worrying about his financial situation, accrue massive wealth, or somebody with Saturn in the fifth may become creatively productive or beget children late in life. Saturn in the tenth may achieve respect and recognition after much concentrated effort.

URANUS

First: Disruption, changeability and eccentricity combine to render an unusual, intelligent and diverse personality, usually with something very striking about the features.

Second: Disruption, changeability and eccentricity are amongst the attitudes projected towards financial status, earning power and values. Brilliant or unusual ideas on how to earn money. Inconsistent values.

Third: Disruption, changeability and eccentricity occur within day-to-day activities. Detached, self-centred relatives. Difficult to educate as a child but extremely bright. Accident-prone when travelling.

Fourth: Disruption, changeability and eccentricity are directed towards the home environment. Many changes of residence. Detached emotions. Uncaring or absent father. Attracted to large, modern decor.

Fifth: Disruption, changeability and eccentricity are channelled into creative outlets, sometimes of a bizarre nature. Unusually gifted but rebellious offspring. Mentally astute with powerful, but erratic physical stamina.

Sixth: Disruption, changeability and eccentricity occur within the working environment. Difficult co-workers. Losses and changes of job. Sudden health problems. Love of unusual or large animals.

Seventh: Disruption, changeability and eccentricity develop during permanent relationships, often causing divorce or separation. Many partners. Either subject or partner will be extremely self-absorbed and independent.

Eighth: Disruption, changeability and eccentricity arise with physical involvement. Unusual sexual desires. Unexpected monetary gains and losses. Detached, unstable emotions. Clever or cunning mind. Occult interests.

Ninth: Disruption, changeability and eccentricity occur when travelling or learning. Changes of religious faith. Brilliant mind. Freedom-seeking. Love of travelling to or learning about exotic, far-away places.

Tenth: Disruption, changeability and eccentricity are channelled into the career, of which there may be more than one. Independent, mind-absorbing career desired. Unfortunate, rebellious or unusual mother.

Eleventh: Disruption, changeability and eccentricity are qualities which friends of this subject possess in abundance. Exciting, unusual group situations attract. Many changes or sudden disappearances of friends.

Twelfth: Disruption, changeability and eccentricity become deeply ingrained within the mind of this individual, sometimes causing mental problems. Unexpected associations with hospitals or institutions.

Note: Despite the fact that Uranus is regarded as being the higher octave of the planet Mercury and therefore basically sexless in character, it does possess many masculine qualities. There is nothing soft, pliable or passive about this strong, magnetic, self-centred planet. The area of the chart in which Uranus is placed will always reveal surprises, upsets, changes and often much talent. It may be beneficial or detrimental in its effect, but never dull or static. It is more at ease when placed in the air or fire signs or in the positive houses – 1st, 3rd, 5th, 7th, 9th and 11th.

NEPTUNE

First: Softness, sensitivity, confusion, and escapism combine to render this person magnetic, ethereal and extremely difficult to understand. Adds a dreamy, far-away look to the features and a round, plump body.

Second: Softness, sensitivity, confusion and escapism are not qualities which auger well for financial success. Losses of money and possessions, or being over-generous or careless with same. Clouded values. Poor appetite.

Third: Softness, sensitivity, confusion and escapism bring about strange events during daily activity. No sense of direction. Mentally confused, disorientated or unhelpful relatives. Lack of concentration in education. Artistic or musical talent.

Fourth: Softness, sensitivity, confusion and escapism create an uneasy home-life with an inability to settle or take root. Strange, absent, negligent or idealised father. Unsure of roots. Chaotic and untidy.

Fifth: Softness, sensitivity, confusion and escapism are all projected into creativity endowing the subject with artistic, musical or theatrical talent. Sensitive or unsettled children. Love of water and liquids, including alcoholic beverages.

Sixth: Softness, sensitivity, confusion and escapism do not make it easy for this person to be confident within a working environment. Strange, undiagnosable health problems. Diabetes or fluid retention a problem. Gentle with animals.

Seventh: Softness, sensitivity, confusion and escapism render it difficult for this subject to find fulfilment within a relationship. Idealisation of partner can occur with eventual disappointment. Unreliable for business partnerships. Attracted to weak or deceitful partners.

Eighth: Softness, sensitivity, confusion and escapism are readily contained and controlled with this placement. Highly emotional and warmly passionate with powerful intuitive faculties. Disappointment through the financial affairs of others, and losses of inheritance or possessions.

Ninth: Softness, sensitivity, confusion and escapism do not blend well into this area. Devoted to religious causes, but can easily be used by stronger people. Travel by sea and studies of a spiritual nature should appeal.

Tenth: Softness, sensitivity, confusion and escapism cause problems of indecision, lack of attainment and self-assertion in this area. Suited to careers of an artistic, musical or theatrical nature. Yearns for recognition but escapist tendencies shun the limelight.

Eleventh: Softness, sensitivity, confusion and escapism render this person kind, sympathetic and helpful towards friends, and prone, therefore, to attracting lame dogs or weak people. Occult, spiritual or religious groups should appeal. Unable to handle responsibility within groups.

Twelfth: Softness, sensitivity, confusion and escapism are hidden qualities of this subject. Neptune copes well in its natural house. Attracted to hospitals and institutions or anything spiritual. Powerful imagination. Regarded as an 'old soul'.

Note: This planet is highly feminine in nature, even though in mythology Neptune was the 'old man of the sea'. Liquids, gases chemicals and oils all fall within Neptune's domain, but the main quality of the planet is its intangibility and lack of substance. People with Neptune strong in their chart are often difficult to pin down, understand or communicate with, sometimes living in a world of their own. All forms of addiction – alcohol, drugs, food, sex – because they are all various forms of escapism – also fall under Neptune's influence. But do be careful when interpreting this nebulous planet, for many strongly Neptunian people appear to be positive, talented and well-adjusted citizens. For example, a person with Neptune in the tenth could be the world's finest musician, actor, dancer or artist, or a totally confused, addicted wreck – or both!

PLUTO

First: Power, authority and magnetism ooze from this subject's personality, sometimes rendering them overbearing and debilitating to others. Tenacity, determination and intensity of features, especially the eyes, will set them apart from the crowd.

Second: Power, authority and magnetism are channelled into earning capacity and financial success. They do not let go of anything with ease. Dedicated to values and prone to obsessive needs.

Third: Power, authority and magnetism are directed towards or received from relatives. Daily activity undertaken with serious, intense concentration. Absorbs information slowly but deeply. Traumatic loss of siblings.

Fourth: Power, authority and magnetism are used within the home. Likes to rule the roost. Early loss of father. Obsessive about home and emotions. Does not take readily to changes of abode.

Fifth: Power, authority and magnetism are exerted over children and loved ones. Strong sexual appeal. Thorough and intense over creative pursuits, but not very adventurous or adaptable. Possible loss of children.

Sixth: Power, authority and magnetism are projected into work situations. Likes to hold positions of respect and command. Extremely capable with animals. Traumatic losses of job. Intense about health, but likely to suffer from growths, or sexual diseases.

Seventh: Power, authority and magnetism are used by one of the partners within a relationship. Traumatic divorce, loss or separation often occurs. Intrinsically loyal and in much need of a firm, steady relationship. Good for business partnerships.

Eighth: Power, authority and magnetism are well controlled in this house. Strong sexual urges, and an innate fascination for the life –

birth/death process, and anthing to do with the underworld. Immense gains or losses through inheritance.

Ninth: Power, authority and magnetism are concentrated into higher learning, religion and travel. Capable of tremendous dedication. Potential for religious leader. May end life in a foreign country or become intense about foreign concerns.

Tenth: Power, authority and magnetism are used within the career. Strongly ambitious with a need for control over others. Good business sense. Careers involving stamina and dedication are suitable. Powerful, dominant mother.

Eleventh: Power, authority and magnetism are projected onto friends and group situations. Desires commanding position within group. Loyal and dependable, yet difficult to approach. Loss of friends.

Twelfth: Power, authority and magnetism are qualities which this subject will only project in his imagination. Intuitive and deep, with a need for some kind of association with hospitals, institutions or prisons, this person is inwardly a loner.

Note: Pluto is regarded as being feminine, because it is basically passive in its energy, but it has much hidden strength, determination and tenacity. Pluto rules volcanoes which can stay dormant for years before erupting. People with Pluto strong in their chart are also like this – capable of controlling virtually all aspects of their character until finally they have to erupt. It is for this reason that Pluto also rules extreme violence and aggression and can even be murderous when roused. The aspects to Pluto are extremely important and can often dominate a whole birth chart. For example, a person with Pluto in the fourth is extremely emotional and intense, but if that Pluto were in square aspect to the Moon, then these qualities would be greatly magnified and capable of causing extreme distress.

When interpreting the planets in houses generally, it is worth noting whether they fall near the beginning or the end of the house. When placed in the first fifteen degrees of a house the planets appear to exert more influence than when placed in the last fifteen degrees. A planet situated within five degrees (approximately) of the following sign usually exhibits many qualities relevant to this sign, e.g., a planet when placed at 14 degrees of Taurus in the seventh house, with the cusp of the eighth being 18 degrees of Taurus, will be influential upon both houses. When very close – within one or two degrees of the next house, the planet will often appear to entirely reflect the qualities of the approaching house.

It is important that you understand the interpretive difference between the planets situated in the signs of the zodiac as compared to the planets situated within the houses of the birth chart. Planets in the signs represent the *mode* (manner of expression) in which we express the various *qualities* of life (planetary energies, or 'drives'). Planets in the houses represent the *area* of life – home, relationships, work, etc. – in which we project the qualities of the planet using the mode of action represented by the sign. For example: Mars in Gemini in the sixth house: the energetic, assertive qualities of Mars will be used within a working, caring, health-conscious environment in an intelligent, adaptable, lively manner.

When you are confident that you can relate to the meanings of the twelve houses, you should answer the following questions in the usual manner.

1. Name the three types of houses.
2. Which house rules romantic attachments, children, creativity, etc?
3. In at least two words describe a person with Mars in the second house.
4. Describe somebody with Saturn in the first house.
5. Which house relates to friends and group situations?
6. Which two houses relate to the mother and father?
7. Which house relates to relationships?
8. What might somebody fear if they had Saturn posited in the eleventh house?
9. How does Jupiter in the tenth like to expand itself?
10. Describe the possible effects of Neptune in the seventh house.

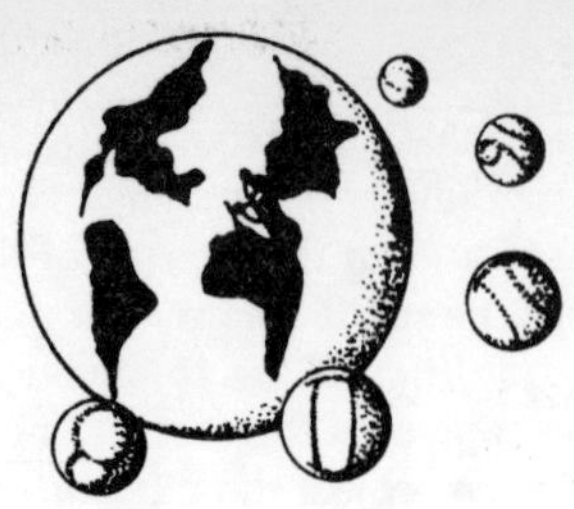

8 · Interpretation: Other Configurations

The signs, houses and aspects are the most influential factors of chart interpretation, but there are many other significant components which can be applied. In this lesson we are going to become acquainted with the most important of these factors.

Chart Shaping

This system of dividing the chart wheel into various distinct types of shapings was originally devised by Marc Edmund Jones and explained in his book *The Guide to Horoscope Interpretation*, which was first published in 1941. Since then it has become an integral part of most astrologers' preliminary interpretation. Diagrams 16 to 23 show the distribution of the original seven shapings plus one extra which commonly appears amongst my file of birth charts.

1. Bundle

A very intense shaping with all planets being contained within 120 degrees, and four or five houses. Gives tenacity, determination and single-minded attitudes to the areas and signs which it occupies,

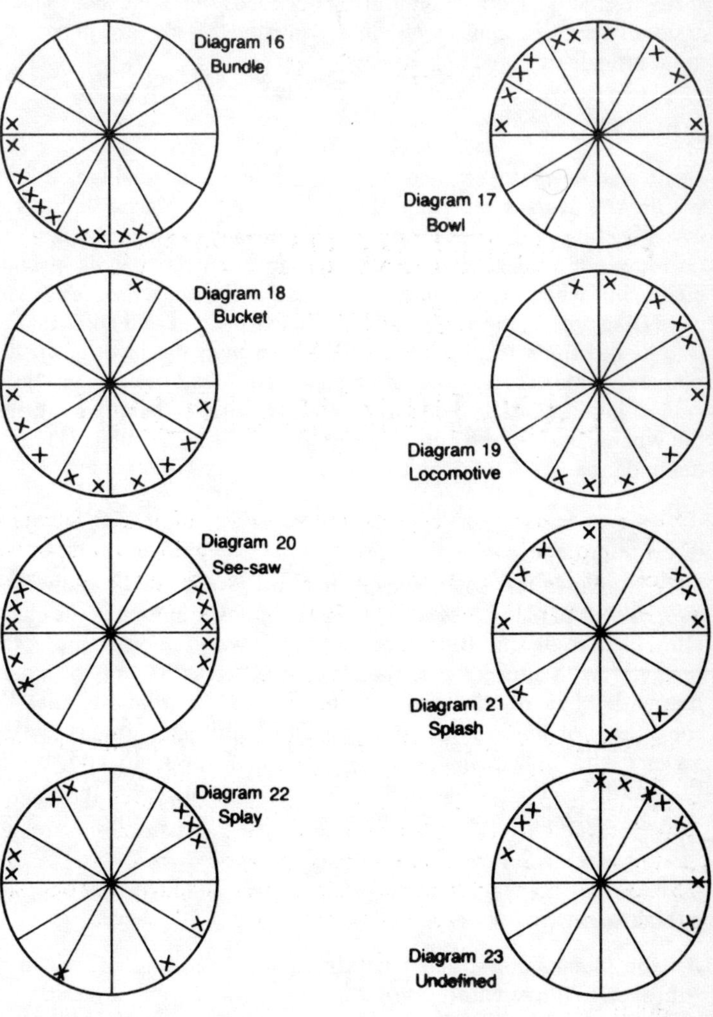
Diagram 16
Bundle
Diagram 17
Bowl
Diagram 18
Bucket
Diagram 19
Locomotive
Diagram 20
See-saw
Diagram 21
Splash
Diagram 22
Splay
Diagram 23
Undefined

being more insular and concerned with personal affairs when in the lower half of the chart and more concerned with public affairs when placed in the upper portion of the chart. Extremely uncommon at the turn of the century but during the 1980s the planets have been gradually aligning themselves closely causing this shaping to become quite prevalent.

2. BOWL

Again a somewhat restricted shaping, all the planets being confined within 180 degrees (one half of the chart). When placed within the lower section of the chart (houses 1–6) the subject is more likely to be introverted, lacking in confidence and concerned with private affairs, but when placed in the upper half of the chart (houses 7–12), as in Diagram 17, the subject is usually extroverted and confident in public, but finds it difficult to relate on a personal level. If all the planets are placed on the ascending half of the chart (houses 10–3) the subject is self-contained and independent, with leadership qualities, but when placed in the opposite half (houses 4–9) the subject is more dependent and often forced to follow the dictates of others.

3. BUCKET

Very similar to the Bowl, except that one planet (or occasionally a conjunction of planets) is situated in the opposite sphere of the chart, allowing a route into the 'other side of the world'. For example, the introvert with nine of his planets in the lower half of the chart, but with Mars in the tenth, is able to emerge from his shell in the sphere of life relating to career and ambition. Conversely, the subject with nine planets in the top half of the chart and one in the fourth, is allowed an access into the personal area of home. The singleton planet is always an extremely important focal point in the life.

4. LOCOMOTIVE

All the planets are situated within 240 degrees (the space of two trines) with the remaining 120 degrees empty. As its name implies, the subject with this shaping has a self-driving personality. The planet leading (pulling) the group in a clockwise direction is said to be the most significant and indicative of the manner in which the subject instigates action, but the planet at the opposite end which appears to be at the rear of the train can often be just as important, especially if it is stronger than the leading planet.

5. SEE-SAW

A shaping which has become uncommon over the last few decades, mainly due to the outer planets aligning themselves close together and rendering it much more difficult for this shape to form. As the name suggests, the planets are divided into two relatively even groups, one in each half of the chart, usually creating several opposition aspects. This shaping causes a permanent striving for balance which is rarely achieved, because, like the motion of the see-saw, the subject veers from one extreme to the other. For example, an extrovert with a need of public recognition (five or six planets in the ninth and tenth) can swiftly change into an introvert with a desperate need for privacy and the mundane personal achievements of life (opposing planets in the third and fourth).

6. SPLASH

In contrast to the first five shapings the Splash shaping reveals planets (usually singletons, but conjunctions are allowable), dotted all over the chart, leaving very few empty houses. The subject with this shaping tends to scatter his interests, being very talented and capable, but finding it difficult to concentrate (similar in effect to the sign of Gemini and the mutable influence). However, because most of the signs, houses, elements, etc., are occupied there is usually much balance, knowledge and understanding of life.

7. SPLAY

Often difficult to differentiate from the Splash, which is similar in appearance, the Splay forms an irregular, uneven type of shaping which tends to occupy a fair amount of the chart. The subject with this shaping finds it difficult or impossible to conform, is independent, unusual and often wilful (the effect can be likened to the planet Uranus or the sign Aquarius).

8. UNDEFINED

Repeatedly within my files I have found a shaping which could not be clearly categorised into any of the above, and decided to name it

'Undefined'. It is reasonably common in births occurring from the sixties onwards. All the planets tend to fall within 210 degrees leaving an approximate space of 150 degrees, therefore being too spread out to be considered a Bowl and not reaching out quite far enough to be considered a Locomotive. It appears to relate strongly to the quincunx aspect and, in common with the aspect much adjustment seems to be required within the subjects' personal lives, which are often difficult, unbalanced or lacking in direction or attainment.

UNOCCUPIED HOUSES

It is all too easy to ignore houses which do not contain planets when interpreting charts, but empty houses contribute almost as much information about a person as occupied houses. Generally speaking, however, the houses which contain planets are the areas of life upon which the subject tends to concentrate, these being either beneficial or detrimental, according to the specific energy of the planet(s) and the aspects involved. Unoccupied houses, on the other hand, concern the areas of life which the subject readily accepts and can operate in with ease, but in which he or she lacks the incentive (a planet) to become committed. For example, a person with no planets in the second will be far less inclined to crave financial security, although they will readily accept its credibility – or somebody with no planets in the seventh will marry, sometimes several times, but cheerfully accept independence and/or a lack of partnerships. When endeavouring to interpret the influence of an unoccupied house it is always extremely enlightening to look to the position of the ruler of the sign on the cusp of the house. Thus if Virgo is on the cusp of an occupied third house, look to see where Mercury is placed, or if Aries is on the cusp of an unoccupied ninth house, find the position of Mars. The position of these rulers gives added information about how the subject relates to the empty house. An empty fourth house, with Taurus on the cusp and Venus placed in the ninth, could indicate that although the home environment is not overly important to the subject, he/she may feel the need for the security of a home when dealing with foreign or learning interests. They may possess a home in a foreign country or feel more 'at home' with people of foreign birth. When studying, they may feel more inclined to do so within their own home environment. In effect, the ninth house will trigger off the fourth house affairs.

Note: This method of interpreting unoccupied houses is not easy for the beginner as it requires much combining of factors, and a complete knowledge of the basics of astrology. Until you are confident in every other respect it would be wise to interpret unoccupied houses only in a general manner as described earlier.

MC (MIDHEAVEN), IC (IMMUM COELI) AND DESCENDANT:

These three points plus the Ascendant, which are calculated according to the time of birth and the position of the Ascendant, form an imaginary cross within the circle of the natal chart. The Midheaven is by far the most important and is regarded as the highest point (a pinnacle of great achievement or satisfaction) within the birth chart. When using the House system explained within this book, the Midheaven can fall anywhere between the 8th and 11th houses, but more commonly within the 9th or 10th houses. The IC is the point which falls in exact opposition to the Midheaven and is therefore regarded as the lowest, innermost part of the chart. It can fall anywhere between the 2nd and 5th houses, but more commonly in the 3rd or 4th. The Descendant is always the cusp (beginning) of the seventh house, and therefore falls at the point exactly opposite the Ascendant (cusp of the first house). Whereas the Ascendant relates entirely to the self, the Descendant depicts how the subject relates to others in close relationships.

RULING PLANET

The planet which rules the sign on the Ascendant is regarded as the ruling planet of the chart and is therefore extremely important. A subject may often present a physical appearance more typical of the sign in which the ruler of the chart is placed than the Ascendant itself. For example, with Gemini on the Ascendant and the ruler Mercury placed in Cancer, the appearance may take on many overtones of a Cancerian. If the ruling planet is in conjunction with another planet, that planet too may affect the appearance. The personality can also be greatly affected by the position of the ruler, and the aspects it makes. If placed in an angular house it may dominate the whole chart. A person with a very extroverted sign such as Leo rising will be more subdued within their personality if the Sun (ruler) falls in a passive sign, whereas a passive, introverted sign rising with the ruler placed in an active sign will generally produce a more confident, outgoing personality. The area of life in which the ruler of the chart falls is highly important and will always be prominent or esteemed.

ANGULAR PLANETS

Any planet falling within an eight degree orb on either side of an angular house, can be regarded as being angular. This includes planets which are situated at the end of the third, sixth, ninth and twelfth houses. For example, a planet situated at 3 degrees of Aquarius in the third house, with the cusp of the fourth at 10 degrees of Aquarius, will still be angular.

Angular planets should be studied carefully, especially when they make many aspects, as they can dominate a chart. They are often indicative of the whole life-style of the subject. For example, Mars angular produces physically active people such as athletes, whereas Neptune angular produces musicians, actors, escapists, addicts, etc.

STELLIUMS

A group of three or more planets posited within one sign or one house is regarded as a stellium. Such a high concentration of planets in one area always indicates tremendous strength, and can therefore govern the chart. The strength may not necessarily be used positively, especially if there are many difficult aspects involved, and the excess of activity within a confined area can often prove to be very difficult to handle. At the time of writing this book (1989) three planets, Saturn, Uranus and Neptune are in the sign of Capricorn, where they will remain until February 1991, when Saturn will leave the fold to enter Aquarius. Therefore, every child born during 1989 and 1990 will possess this stellium in one (or perhaps two) of the twelve houses, thereby raising the potential (unless well aspected) to cause the subject a great deal of stress in the area, or areas, of life concerned. If the planets in the stellium are well spread, for example one at 2 degrees of a sign and two more at the end of the same sign, they will usually occupy two consecutive houses and the influence will be slightly lessened.

PLANETS IN EXALTATION, DETRIMENT AND FALL

The original seven planets are traditionally considered to be exalted (well-placed) when posited in certain signs, as follows:

☉ is exalted in ♈
☽ is exalted in ♉
☿ is exalted in ♍
♀ is exalted in ♓
♂ is exalted in ♑
♃ is exalted in ♋
♄ is exalted in ♎

When these same planets are placed in the signs opposite those above they are considered to be in their 'fall' (weakly placed). For example, the Sun is in its fall in Libra.

A planet is considered to be in detriment when placed in the sign opposite to that which it rules. For example, Venus rules both Taurus and Libra and is therefore supposedly in detriment (badly placed) when in the signs of Scorpio and Aries. A planet in its own sign, however, is considered to be strong.

Although it is worth noting these traditional placements, caution should be applied when using them in interpretation, as they are often inappropriate. For example Jupiter exalted in Cancer may very well produce a person with remarkably positive Cancerian qualities, but it could also produce an excess of sensitivity, vulnerability, protective attitudes and emotion. Mars, however, which is supposedly in its fall when placed within Cancer, could easily produce similar positive effects to those attributed to Jupiter.

RETROGRADE PLANETS

When retrograde, planets *appear* to be moving backwards when seen from an earth perspective and this apparent motion backwards is obviously at the root of the belief that retrograde planets are less effective within a birth chart than those which are moving direct. (Note: The Sun and Moon never turn retrograde.) This assumption seems to possess little credibility, especially with the outer planets which, because they move so slowly are often retrograde for great periods. It has been noted, however, that when Mercury turns retrograde delays, frustrations and confusion over all Mercurial concerns seem to occur. Post is delayed, transport is inefficient, and daily communication may be beset with problems. People with Mercury retrograde in their birth chart frequently possess some kind of communication problem. Venus retrograde often finds it difficult to love, and Mars retrograde may have problems in expelling energy. It is therefore well worth noting when these three personal planets are retrograde within a birth chart.

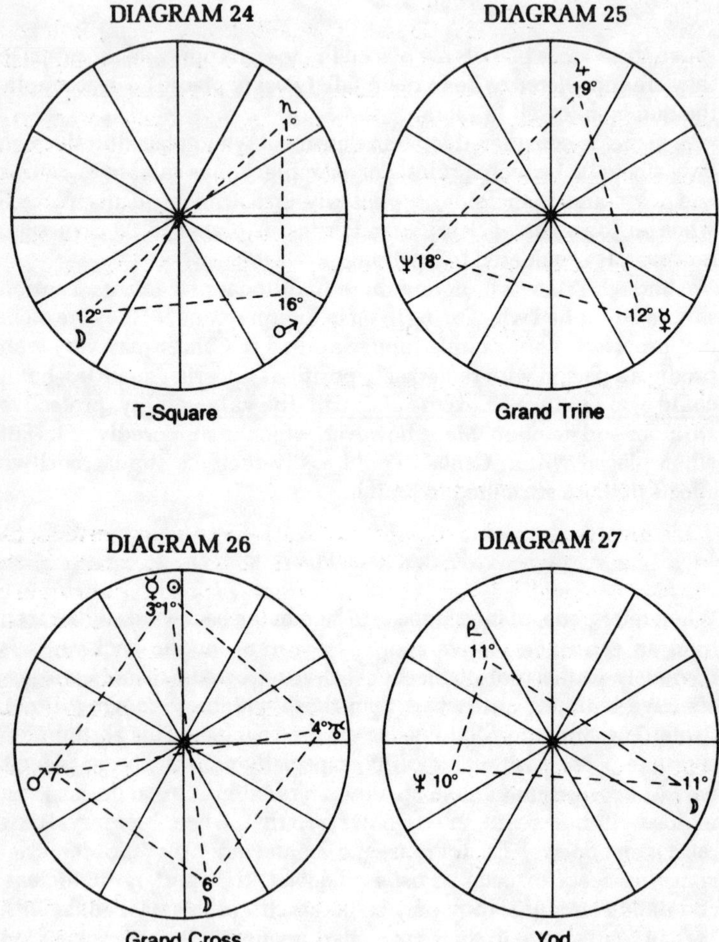
DIAGRAM 24
♄ 1°
12° ☽
16° ♂
T-Square
DIAGRAM 25
♃ 19°
♆ 18°
12° ☿
Grand Trine
DIAGRAM 26
☿ ☉ 3° 1°
4° ♅
♂ 7°
6° ☽
Grand Cross
DIAGRAM 27
♇ 11°
♆ 10°
11° ☽
Yod

UNASPECTED PLANETS

A planet that does not form any aspects with another planet is regarded as unaspected, although it may still form aspects to the Ascendant and Midheaven.

Any unaspected planet must be regarded as a strong influence for either good or ill, simply because it represents completely pure, unmitigated energy – an energy that is abundant and flowing freely. Sometimes, however, there may be too much energy and the unaspected planet may be prone to uncontrollable excesses. For example, unaspected Mars could indicate a powerful physical stamina or athletic prowess, which if abused or uncontrolled may lead to excessive anger or violence. Unaspected Moon may be either highly protective and nurturing or oversensitive and clinging.

MAJOR PLANETARY CONFIGURATIONS

These consist of various groupings of several major aspects as follows:

THE T-SQUARE: ☍ (SEE DIAGRAM 24)

This involves a combination of two squares and an opposition, the two planets involved in the opposition both being square to the third planet, which forms the 'T'. It is a very common configuration, renowned for its difficulty and lack of ease in operating. The subjects are often very tense and lacking in fulfilment within the areas occupied by the planets. Much hard work and understanding is required in order to render the configuration harmonious and productive in its energy. Three or more planets can be involved, but if more than three, there must be at least one close conjunction of two or more of the planets.

THE GRAND TRINE: △ (SEE DIAGRAM 25)

A combination of three trines involving three or more planets (more than three planets must also involve a conjunction of at least two planets), usually within the same element, form this major figure. Regarded as being highly beneficial and easy to operate, it also appears to add charm, lightness and talent to the birth chart. As with all trines, however, there is a tendency for inertia or acceptance, thereby nullifying the tremendous advantages of the configuration.

THE GRAND CROSS: + (SEE DIAGRAM 26)

Far less common than the T-Square and Grand Trine, this powerful configuration involves at least four planets combined in four squares and two oppositions and forming an imaginary cross shape upon the chart. With six difficult aspects involved it is inevitably an extremely problematical configuration to conquer and use wisely. It often brings tremendous conflicts and difficulties into the lives of its owners, becoming even more potent when angular or placed in the angular houses. The subjects tend to make the same mistakes over and over again. They easily become obsessed, aggressive and rebellious, or depressed, escapist and self-abasing, according to the planets and signs involved. However, once the awesome power of this configuration is harnessed, controlled and channelled in the right direction, there is very little that the subject cannot achieve.

THE YOD ▷ (SEE DIAGRAM 27)

Also known as the Finger of God, this is the least common of the four major configurations. It involves two quincunxes and a sextile, the two planets creating the sextile both making a quincunx to the third planet, and thereby forming a pointed finger shape. The planet involved in the two quincunxes is considered to be the focal point of release for the other two planets, its skill and talents being better utilised with the aid of the remaining two planets. Occasionally one or more extra planets are involved in this configuration, but as both the quincunx and sextile use smaller orbs than the aspects involved in the other configurations, it is quite a rare phenomenon. The Yod does seem to indicate a 'special' gift or talent which should be used by the individual, but in common with the quincunx aspect the talent may not be apparent, or utilised until much adjustment has been made and time elapsed. The configuration usually occurs in the charts of highly developed, or spiritual individuals.

THE MOON'S NODES

North Node ☊ South Node ☋

Traditionally referred to as the Dragon's Head (North Node) and the Dragon's Tail (South Node) these are two astronomical points of the Moon's orbit as it crosses the ecliptic from South to North (forming the North Node) and from North to South (forming the South Node). Their influence in the birth chart is rarely devastating, but is worthy of attention. They are often regarded as being concerned with life's lessons as brought about by karma. The South Node supposedly represents the talents, abilities and habits brought forward from a previous lifetime, which the subject tends to use freely and resort to in times of stress. The North Node, on the other hand, is thought to represent the present karma – the main area of life in which progress should be made. The sign occupied by the North Node is indicative of the manner in which we should strive to reach the required goals. It is often difficult for a person to use their North Node in favour of their South Node.

The Moon's Nodes also seem pertinent within relationships. When two birth charts are compared for their compatibility (a branch of astrology called synastry) a connection (exact aspect) between the Nodes of one person to the planet(s) of the other is often present.

All the above facets of astrology are important and should be digested, learned and applied with care.

The following questions are very diverse, but do treat them in the normal manner, and do not move on until you are able to answer at least seven questions satisfactorily.

1. In our Example chart No. 4 (refer back to Diagram 7) what is the ruling planet?
2. In the same chart list any angular planets you can see.
3. Referring to the aspect grids for our five examples on page 50, can you see if there are any unaspected planets?
4. If the Sun, Jupiter, Neptune and Pluto were all in the sign of Scorpio, what would they be forming?
5. In which signs are Saturn and Mars exalted?
6. Explain how a Bowl shaping is identified, and its meaning.
7. How might a Grand Trine manifest itself?
8. In which sign is Jupiter in its fall?
9. The fact of being retrograde rather than direct is of more importance, in terms of interpretation, for some planets than others. Which ones?
10. The MC in Diagram 8 is at 15 degrees of Aquarius. Where would the IC be situated?

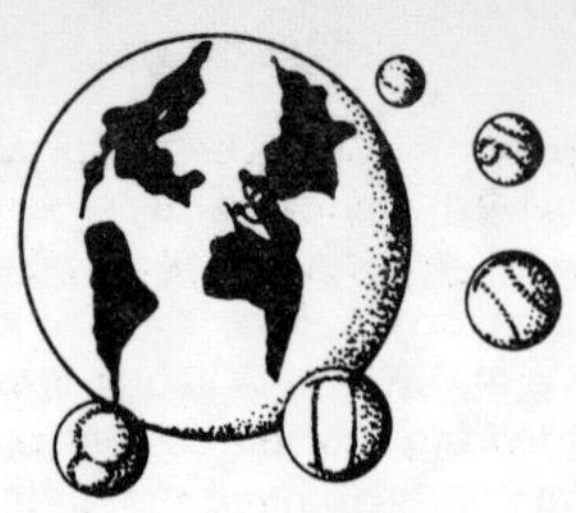

9·PREDICTIVE ASTROLOGY:

Moving on from the analysis of a birth chart, the next step is to learn about the predictive element of astrology (the effect of the continuous movement of the planets upon our lives). There are many alternative methods of prognosis, but this lesson will deal purely with the two traditionally esteemed methods – Progressions and Transits, for which you will require a copy of an ephemeris which covers up to the year 2000.

PROGRESSIONS

A relatively simple, precise method of prediction in which the personal planets, Sun, Moon, Mercury, Venus and Mars play the vital role. These planets are progressed within the ephemeris 'a day for each year', in the following manner.

Turn to the relevant date of birth in the ephemeris, then count down each day until you arrive at the day which corresponds to the actual age, moving onto the following month or page, if necessary. For example, for sixteen years of age count on sixteen days, for fifty years of age count on fifty days. The planet's positions on this new date are the progressed positions for the birthday of the year in question, but they require minor adjustments before being used for predictive purposes. To demonstrate we shall use our example No. 2, who was born at 9.40 p.m. Greenwich Mean Time on 6 July 1941. To find out the progressed planet's positions for this subject upon attaining the age of 21, count down twenty-one days from 6 July to arrive at the date of 27 July, then using the GMT birthtime of 9.40 p.m. make slight adjustments as follows.

The position of the Sun at noon on 27 July 1941 is 4 degrees 2 minutes Leo. As our subject was born after midday a small amount of time needs to be added on. Applying the same system of adjustment used in Lesson 4, (the Sun moving one degree per day), we need to add approximately 24 minutes to the Sun's position, thereby making it 4 degrees 26 minutes of Leo. Using the same procedure of adjustment for daily movement as learnt in Lesson 4, work out any necessary rectifications for the planets Moon, Mercury, Venus and Mars. Having done so, you should arrive at the following figures.

Sun	4 degrees 26 minutes Leo	Positions of planets for 6/7/1963
Moon	18 degrees Virgo (approximately)	
Mercury	15 degrees 03 minutes Virgo	
Venus	0 degrees 52 minutes Virgo	
Mars	13 degrees 25 minutes Aries	

When working out the progressed positions for any other time of the year a few further adjustments are required, mainly to the Moon, which in progression moves approximately one degree per month and takes two and a half years to travel through one sign or house. To find the degree of the progressed Moon for any given month in the year, simply add on one degree per month from the date of birth, or subtract one degree per month for any month prior to the birth. For example, the position of the Moon in December 1963, for our subject will have progressed five degrees (August to December) and therefore be at 23 degrees of Virgo. The Moon's position in February 1963, however, would have been five degrees less than eighteen degrees (March to July) and therefore be at thirteen degrees Virgo. Only the Moon requires any major adjustment, but always check the remaining planets to see how fast they are moving, remembering that the daily motion of planets corresponds to a year in progressions. So, for example if Mercury is moving nearly three degrees per day, this represents three degrees per year.

In summary therefore, the following formula applies when working out progressions.

1. Count down in the ephemeris the number of days corresponding to the age of the subject.
2. Work across using the GMT time at birth to calculate in the same manner

as the natal birth chart, the exact positions of the subject's progressed planets (Sun to Mars).

3. Make any necessary adjustments for the time of year in which the prediction is taking place, remembering that the movement of the planets is correspondingly slowed down, the Sun moving one degree per year, the Moon approximately twelve degrees per year, Mercury variable between 0 and 3 degrees per year, Venus variable between 0 and 2 degrees per year and Mars rarely moving more than 1 degree per year.

Note: Because they move so slowly, the three outer planets are rarely used in progressions. It is however worth keeping an eye on Jupiter and Saturn, especially from middle age onwards as they may have progressed a few degrees and should therefore be used within the interpretation.

The Ascendant can also be progressed, and a progressed birth chart erected if desired. To progress the Ascendant use the sidereal time of the new date – in our example case the sidereal time at noon on 27 July 1941, and calculate the new Ascendant in exactly the same manner as for a natal birth chart using the subject's actual birth time. Then place in the planets for the new date using the same system as in Lesson 4.

The interpretation of progressed planets is relatively easy. The new positions of the planets are placed on the birth chart (preferably near to the centre of the chart) and then related to the natal chart, noting any change of house or sign, and any new aspects being formed. Due to their very slow movement, however, and the length of time it takes the planets (apart from the Moon) to traverse a few degrees, only a very small orb of 1–2 degrees is allowable for any aspect.

Using our example chart (turn to Diagram 5 on page 36) and the calculations for the 21st year as above, we note that progressed Sun at 4 degrees of Leo is situated exactly between (at the midpoint of) Pluto and Venus in Leo, causing a major progression and therefore an important turning-point in the subject's life. Any progressed aspect to Pluto results in transformation, change and the end of an old way of life, whilst progressed aspects to Venus can bring about love, a heightened sense of values and a desire for materialistic security. In our subject's case the two planets are in the sixth house of work and health so the progressed Sun aspect (conjunction) will affect this area of life. A major change of job or place of work could be applicable, with the combining effect of a new, potent love relationship, which may, or may not be the cause of the situation. (Progressed Sun conjunct natal Venus on the Descendant.)

Progressed Moon in the eighth house reaches 19 degrees of Virgo in

August (using the one degree a month formula) and forms a square to natal Moon in the eleventh house, causing possible emotional upsets with friendships and the financial security of loved ones.

Progressed Mercury at 15 degrees of Virgo in the eighth house is not making any aspects, but in 1964 makes a square to natal Moon in the eleventh causing further communication problems or challenges with friends or groups situations.

Progressed Venus at 0–1 degree of Virgo is in the seventh house and not forming any aspects.

Progressed Mars at 13 degrees of Aries in the third house is not making any aspects but during 1964 forms a square to the Sun at 14 degrees of Cancer in the sixth house. Arguments or conflicts at work, or health problems relating to the head (Mars in Aries), heart (the Sun) or stomach (the sign Cancer) could arise from this aspect.

GENERAL NOTES ON PROGRESSIONS

Due to the slowness of movement of progressed planets all aspects must be kept to a maximum 1–2 degree orb.

Changes of houses or sign occur very infrequently (for example, once every thirty years for the Sun) and are therefore extremely important.

Progressed planets changing signs can cause subtle changes of character. Thus, a person born with the Sun in Leo will become more earthy and mutable when their progressed Sun enters the sign of Virgo, or somebody born with Mercury in sensitive Cancer will become more confident in their communication when progressed Mercury enters the sign of Leo.

Generally speaking all aspects formed by progressed planets to natal planets will manifest in a very similar manner to natal aspects. For example, squares may prove challenging, whereas trines are usually harmonious. A conjunction of progressed Sun to natal Venus should be a loving or creative time, whereas progressed Sun to natal Mars will be more energetic, dynamic and possibly aggressive or violent.

When a progressed planet enters an empty house it will remain in that area for quite some time, thereby helping to bring that area to life and creating a tremendous impact on what was once an area of disinterest.

Exact progressed Moon aspects last for approximately one month and basically form a monthly cycle of development. Individually these aspects seldom create great trauma or action but in combination with other major progressions they will act as an emotional trigger and intensify the situation.

TRANSITS

The method of using the daily orbiting transits of the planets in predictive astrology is the easiest and most effective system of all. Quite simply, it entails referring to the ephemeris for any given date in order to find the position of the planets on that day, and then checking to see how they relate to the birth chart.

The five outermost planets, Jupiter to Pluto, are far more important than the personal planets when predicting major events. The personal planets, because of their speed of movement, are better utilised for daily or weekly interpretations on a mundane level.

Using our subject who was born on 6 July 1941, as our example once again, we can turn to any date in any year listed in the ephemeris to find out how the transiting planets will affect his life. To find out what is happening on 6 July 1989 (his 48th birthday) we must turn to the relevant page in the ephemeris for this date and look across at the position of the planets, commencing with the planet Pluto, which is situated at 12 degrees of Scorpio, retrograde, and when placed in the subject's birth chart falls in the otherwise empty tenth house of career, aims and ambitions, adding stimulus and incentive to this area of his life. It does not form any exact major aspects and can therefore be considered to be working on a reasonably positive level.

Moving left across the page we note Neptune's position to be at 10 degrees retrograde of Capricorn, which when placed in our subject's birth chart falls once again in an empty house – this time the twelfth. Outer planets transiting the twelfth house can sometimes be very problematical, particularly when the house is natally empty. Over-imagination, sacrifices, guilts and secrets can cause depression or unhappiness. When any planets are transiting through the twelfth it is an excellent time to take stock of life and endeavour to improve the spiritual qualities, by helping others and sacrificing any excessively materialistic attitudes. Neptune is not making any major aspects and will not do so until it forms an opposition with the Sun in Cancer at 14 degrees, in March–April 1990 (check with the ephemeris for these months to see Neptune at 14 degrees of Capricorn).

Moving to the left once more we find Uranus placed at 2 degrees retrograde of Capricorn and therefore situated in our subject's eleventh house of friends and group activities, forming an exact square aspect to Mars at 2 degrees of Aries. Challenges and upsets to the subject's finances and values (second house) could therefore occur through unreliable, erratic friends or group situations (Uranus in the eleventh).

Saturn is at ten degrees retrograde of Capricorn, moving down to nine then eight degrees by the end of the month. It remains in our subject's twelfth house, having entered in the middle of January 1989 (check back in the ephemeris to note this change of house), and makes aspects to both Jupiter (a quincunx) and Mercury (an opposition). The quincunx, in transit, is rarely serious and will only create minor stress in the areas which the two planets occupy. The opposition to Mercury is more forceful and operating from the twelfth house of hospitals to the sixth house of health there could well be a spell of health problems or mental depression. Added responsibility or burdens at work (the sixth house) which is an extremely important area for our subject (note the stellium in this house) could also occur.

Transiting Jupiter usually moves fairly quickly and only forms exact aspects for four to five days at a time. On 6 July 1989 it is at 24 degrees of Gemini and therefore placed in our subject's fifth house, hopefully adding benefits within this area – romance, creativity, children, gambling and sports should all prove worthwhile, especially when Jupiter makes good aspects. Looking closely we see that it does in fact form a square to Neptune from approximately 7 to 12 January. Neptune in its negative form indicates escapes and losses and Jupiter when challenged by a square indicates excess, so this brief aspect could predict losses of other people's finances (note that Neptune is situated in the eighth house) or negligent over-optimistic attitudes with children or loved ones.

Judging from the quantity of these challenging aspects, with very few easy ones to mitigate the effect, our subject appears to be going through a difficult spell but if he meets the challenges by relating positively to the planetary energies he will eventually reap the rewards. Negative reactions however will enable the planets to wreak havoc and disruption.

GENERAL NOTES ON TRANSITS

Planets in transit are much more dynamic and instant in their effect than planets in progression.

A transiting planet is extremely powerful when changing from one house to another, especially when moving into an unoccupied house. The sign, however, has much less bearing upon personal lives.

Due to the retrograde action of the planets some aspects are formed several times within a year (or two, when Pluto is moving at its slowest). The initial forming of the aspect is usually the most powerful, but sometimes the very last return of the aspect can be the most crucial.

The transiting energy of the planets is very similar to that projected in the natal charts. Pluto will cause volcanic eruption, transformation and trauma. Neptune will create confusion, chaos, misunderstanding, losses, escapism, spiritual feelings, idealism and creativity. Uranus will generate excitement, sudden change, rebellion, unusual events and a need for independence. Saturn will precipitate burdens, responsibilities, depression, tiredness, frustration, steadiness and stability and provide karmic lessons in life. Jupiter will bring about benefits, excesses, liberation, luck, optimism, cheerfulness, over-confidence and sometimes unruliness.

When looking at the personal planets, the current position of Mars will signify the area in which much of the present energy is being expended. Venus will denote an area of temporary harmony and peace. Mercury shows the area in which communication is likely to occur and the Sun provides ego, strength and a sense of purpose to whichever house it is occupying.

Conjunctions are the most potent of transiting aspects, their effect being twice as strong as a square, opposition or trine.

Some people do not respond very noticeably to any transiting aspects, whereas others respond to the slightest stimulus. Those with many difficult aspects within their natal birth charts are more likely to feel the effects of transiting aspects, especially if the transiting aspect is repeating an aspect from the birth chart. In our example's birth chart Saturn is conjunct Uranus. Several times during 1988 these two planets were once again in conjunction. Our subject would almost certainly have experienced this aspect in a forceful manner.

The hypothesis that any planet can operate negatively or positively within a birth chart, also applies to transits, but it can be very difficult to harness the potent energy of the three outermost planets, Uranus, Neptune and Pluto, especially if they are difficultly aspected within the birth chart.

Transiting aspects can manifest in a multitude of ways, and it is not easy to pinpoint exactly what will happen to a subject – one can only outline several indications of direction. Thus Uranus transiting the fifth house could encourage sudden, exciting romantic affairs, or induce children to behave rebelliously. It could also give tremendous potential for startling, exciting creative activity. It may even spur the subject into taking up a new hobby such as flying or computer studies (both ruled by Uranus). In some charts a planet transiting a house will bring about many differing incidents, whereas the same planet in another chart will react very mildly with one main occurrence. All this variance does make it very difficult to predict specific events in astrology. A good astrologer, however, should be able to give a reasonably accurate idea of future trends.

Endeavour to interpret the effects of both progressed and transiting planets as you would for a natal chart, remembering that the effects are indeed transitory, unlike the positions of the planets in the natal chart.

MAJOR PLANETARY CYCLES

Planets vary in the length of time it takes them to travel through the birth chart and form their own cycles:

PLUTO

Because Pluto moves extremely slowly and somewhat erratically, taking between ten and thirty years to travel through one sign or house, it is impossible for any person to experience a complete cycle of this tiny planet. It may only transit two or three signs or houses within a life-time. Therefore, the movement of Pluto from one house into another signifies a vitally transforming period of life. The aspects Pluto forms whilst in transit must always be observed very carefully as no other planet is capable of causing quite so much devastation and trauma when operating negatively.

NEPTUNE

Neptune, too, moves very slowly (changing signs approximately once every fourteen years) and will seldom, therefore, move more than five or six signs or houses throughout a lifetime. The major aspect Neptune forms during its long cycle is the square to natal Neptune which occurs during the early to middle forties and coincides with the mid-life crisis. It can often be a confusing, disorientating time with a desire for a change of direction in life.

URANUS

The Uranus cycle is speedier (seven years to transit a sign or house). It is possible to experience this planet's return to its natal (birth) position, at around the age of 84. This cycle is called a Uranus Return. Many people who survive to the age of 84 experience a most unexpected new lease of life at this time. The second, if not the most important event in the Uranus cycle is the Uranus half return (when Uranus opposes its natal birth position), which occurs anytime between the late thirties and early forties. This aspect, too, coincides with the onset of middle age and often causes much disruption, rebellion and search for independence. Women especially feel the urge to be free and seek out drastic changes within their previously secure lives. It is very much a time for coming to terms with one's own needs and creative outlets. Uranus square Uranus, which occurs between the ages of 19 and 21, is a similar period of seeking one's own identity and freedom.

SATURN

Saturn's cycle is much faster – it takes only two and a half years for this planet to travel through one sign or house, and therefore twenty-eight to thirty years for it to reach the same position it occupied at birth (the first Saturn Return). Between the ages of 56 and 58 Saturn returns for the second time, and for a third time (if you are lucky) at approximately 87. The first Saturn return is regarded as the most significant, and its effects are extremely diverse, applying to almost anything from a broken marriage, a birth of a child, a severe period of depression or a profound spell of creativity. Marriages, too, are extremely common during this time.

Saturn is regarded as a teacher, and if we learn our lessons well we are duly rewarded. There are some people, however, who make the same mistakes over and over again, and these people often have Saturn dominant in their chart. They appear to be afraid of moving in the right direction, of taking chances in life and giving up their strong material instincts. If the required lessons have not been learnt by the end of the first Saturn Return the second can be equally traumatic.

JUPITER

Jupiter takes approximately one year to travel through one sign or house and twelve years to complete its cycle. The first Jupiter return at around the age of 12 marks a turning-point in one's physical development, the second, at approximately 24, in one's emotional development, and the third, at 36, in one's creative development. The fourth, at the age of 48, heralds the onset of middle age. Each twelve-year cycle indicates a major expansion in one's life and is usually an important, uplifting time.

SUN, MOON, MERCURY, VENUS AND MARS

All these planets have important cycles, the Sun 30 days, (and one year), the Moon 28 days, Mercury, Venus and Mars variable, which are influential on a day-to-day basis, but nowhere so intense in their effect as the outer planets.

The above has been a brief introduction to the workings of progressions and transits. Read the lesson through several times and map out the movement of the planets within your own chart before attempting the questions below.

1. Which planets are the most important when dealing with progressions?
2. If a person were 52 years of age how many days would you count on from the date of birth in the ephemeris to find the progressed positions?
3. How long does it take the progressed Sun to travel through one sign or house?
4. Which is the fastest-moving progressed planet and roughly approximately how many degrees does it travel in a year?
5. Which planets are considered the most important when working with transits?
6. At what age does the first Saturn Return occur?
7. What effect might transiting Uranus have in the tenth house?
8. Which aspect is the most important when analysing transits?
9. How often does one experience a Jupiter return?
10. If a person had progressed Mercury entering an empty fourth house, how would you expect them to relate to this movement?

10 · Sample Analysis: Charles Dickens

In this, the final stage of our ten-lesson course, the complete analysis of a birth chart is delineated. Every astrologer has their own particular method of interpretation. It is vital that you choose a system which you find easy and enjoyable, and then adhere to it.

The following interpretation of the birth chart of Charles Dickens (Diagram 28) is presented in a manner which I have used for many years. Divided into two sections, the first encompasses the overview (broad outline) of the chart and covers elements, quadruplicities, aspects, etc., and any unusual or striking qualities about the chart, and the second systematically proceeds through each house interpreting the planets (or lack of planets) therein. The system is orderly, simple and fully comprehensive. I suggest that whilst in the process of learning you use this method in order to gain full advantage of the previous lessons.

1. The Broad Outline of the Chart

Chart Shaping

Dickens' chart is nearest to a Bucket-type shaping. Jupiter – the only planet situated in the top half of the circle is regarded as a handle to the shaping, and therefore a very important planet. With nine planets posited in the lower (personal) section of his chart, Dickens tended to

DIAGRAM 28
CHARLES DICKENS
Born Midnight, 7.2.1812
Portsmouth, Hants

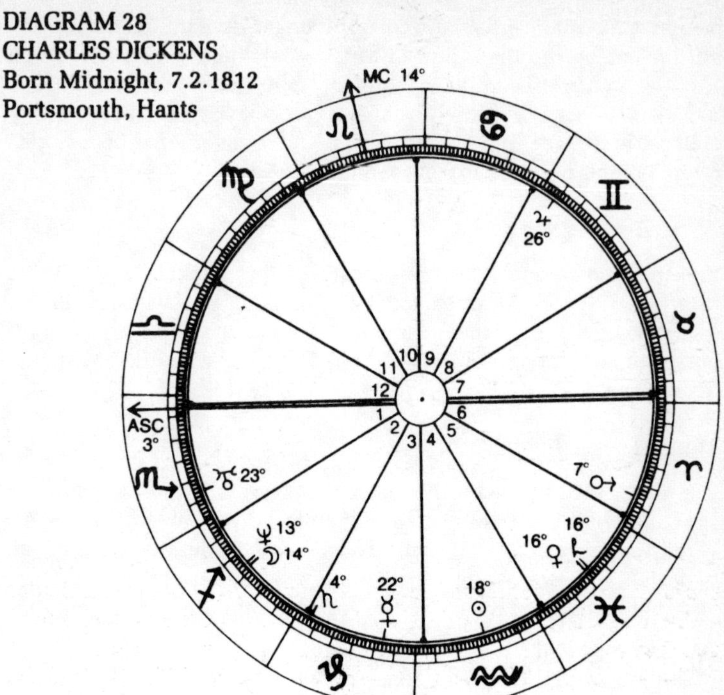

Active	5
Passive	5
Fire	3 (+MC)
Earth	2
Air	2
Water	3 (+ASC)
Cardinal	3
Fixed	2
Mutable	5
Ruling planet	♇
Ruler's house	5th
Angular	Nil
Chart shaping	Bucket

☉⚹☽	
☉⚺♀	ASC. △♃
☉△♃	ASC. ⚹♄
☉□♅	MC. ☍☉
☉⚺♇	MC. △☽
☽□♀	MC. ⚻♀
☽△♂	
☽☌♆	MC. △♂
☽□♇	MC. △♆
☿⚹♅	MC. ⚻♆
♀△♅	
♀□♆	
♀☌♇	
♂□♄	
♅△♇	
♆□♇	

be a very private, selfish and insular person in many realms of life, but fortunately, Jupiter allowed him a vital channel through which his energy could be utilised within public spheres. Jupiter placed in Mercury-ruled Gemini – the sign of writing expanded his writing abilities and made him a prominent figure. In later years he was also renowned for being an excellent public speaker.

ACTIVE/PASSIVE RATIO

Five planets in each division, indicates that Dickens was able to keep the balance between extrovertism and introvertism. In his own personally orientated manner he was capable of grasping all angles of a situation – an ability which was readily utilised within his writing.

THE ELEMENTS

These are well-balanced. Fire and water are slightly stronger and the combination of these two elements helped to emphasise his volatile, highly emotional, enthusiastic and restless tendencies, all of which, however, were usually stabilised by his strong Capricorn and intellectualised by his Sun in Aquarius and Jupiter in Gemini.

THE QUADRUPLICITIES

A slight imbalance towards mutable rendered him restless, changeable and adaptable. Desipte the low fixed quadruplicity, Dickens was able to sustain his literary efforts well and produce excellent work. In this respect he was certainly aided by the effects of Saturn and Mercury in the third house (writing and communication) in the indomitable sign of Capricorn, and also by the fixed angles of his chart.

ASPECT PATTERNS AND OTHER CONSIDERATIONS

There are no angular planets in Dickens' chart – a fact which tends to give the planets equality in strength, and endows the subject with a complex character. Saturn and Mars are situated in the sign they rule, giving them extra force and energy, which is accentuated by the square aspect they make to one another – an aspect of frustrated energy and aggression which can often cause emotional and/or health problems.

Venus is exalted in Pisces and conjunct the ruler of the chart – Pluto, adding intensity and power to his love-life, which was immensely important to him. Both the Sun and Jupiter are in detriment, but this supposedly debilitating influence seemed to have little effect, as both planets operated with strength in his chart.

Mercury and Saturn only form one aspect each – Mercury a sextile to Uranus and Saturn a square to Mars, thereby making these two aspects particularly strong, and highlighting once again the Capricorn and third house factors of his chart. The Mercury–Uranus sextile rendered Dickens stimulating, exciting and mentally brilliant and he was able to use these characteristics within his writing.

The powerful Moon, Venus and Pluto aspects show his passionate need for love, security and release of emotions, but also a desire to control the feelings of others and bend them to his will.

2. HOUSE INTERPRETATION

FIRST HOUSE

With Scorpio on the Ascendant and Uranus in Scorpio in the first house, Dickens' personality was intense, emotional, possessive and hypnotic (Scorpio), and exciting, erratic, eccentric, rebellious and obstinate (Uranus). He would rarely admit that he was wrong or accede to any unsatisfactory situation, yet he was extremely popular and warm-hearted when happy. Such is the magnetic strength of this Uranus–Scorpio combination. The ruler of the Ascendant, Pluto, conjunct Venus in Pisces in the fifth helped enormously in this respect and added to his mesmeric power – he actually practised hypnotising his wife and comrades in an attempt to heal them of their ailments and was reasonably successful in doing so. But whenever he was challenged the cold, hard and wilful detachment of Uranus in the first in the controlling sign of Scorpio would come to the fore and he exhibited an extremely formidable exterior.

His appearance was typical of a water sign rising. He was not particularly tall, and fairly stout in his later years. His eyes were dreamy, rounded and sensitive in youth – more typical of the sign Pisces (ruler of the Ascendant situated in Pisces) but in later years they became harder and deeper more in line with his Scorpio Ascendant.

SECOND HOUSE:

Money, financial status and possessions were undoubtedly of paramount importance to Dickens throughout his life. In his early years it was the stigma of never having enough. His parents were always in debt and could not control their financial affairs. Much of Dickens' childhood was spent in poverty and he therefore became acutely aware of the need for financial security from a very tender age (Moon in the second house). The strong Scorpio and Capricorn elements of his birth chart gave him sensibility, cautiousness and shrewdness when handling his monetary affairs in later life, but the Neptune-Moon conjunction in Sagittarius always seemed to work against him. He spent much of his life paying off other people's debts (the ruler of the second, Jupiter, in the eighth house of other people's finances) and swiftly spending his hard-earned cash on family and travel. The Moon in the second gave him financial security but Neptune – the planet of losses and escapism – allowed much of it to slip through his fingers.

THIRD HOUSE

This is probably the most important area of Dickens' life because it has much to do with his writing talents. All the cadent houses can represent communication through writing, but more especially the third and the ninth. Dickens' third house is extremely strong and the planet Jupiter is reaching out towards his ninth. Mercury in Capricorn relates to his imagination and desire to communicate in a serious, steady manner, accentuated greatly by Saturn, which gave him stability, dedication and at times a certain morbidity and fearfulness which he portrayed in his characters. These planets also rendered his speech harsh (Saturn), speedy and stilted (Mercury), especially during his youth. Jupiter in Gemini (denoting fluency of speech) helped to mitigate these effects, however, and in later years he became a very good public speaker.

The third house also relates to siblings, of which he had many and to whom he was close. One of his younger brothers was like a son to him, but several of his family proved to be burdens whom he supported and maintained for much of their lives with a dedicated sense of duty and responsibility which only a chart strong in Capricorn could understand.

Any planets in the third house render the native restless and in need of daily stimulation, preferably mental. In Dickens' case he also enjoyed physical activity. He would walk for miles, and possessed a great attunement to the land (Capricorn, earth).

The S
the c
diffic
eithe
his
rule
his
the
to

I
pa
hi
av
fr
th
h
f
t

Dickens
powerfully in all fifth house
creative, imaginative and emotionally intense – the serious
relating to Capricorn and the escapist sentimental factors to Pisces.

Dickens was also a keen actor (the fifth house, the signs Pisces and Leo, and the planet Neptune often denote an attraction to acting). In his youth he performed and mimicked to his family, whilst in his adulthood he directed plays and formed his own private acting companies which he ruled and dominated with his usual powerful magnetism (Venus conjunct Pluto). At one stage during his adolescence he decided to take up acting as a career (Leo on the cusp of the tenth house of career) but this failed to work out.

Within his love-life Dickens was romantic, intense and obsessive. He loved deeply and formed many liaisons throughout his life, even whilst married, but many of them were purely platonic or spiritual attachments (Pisces). He needed romance as much as the earth needs rain. In his early years he lacked confidence in this respect (the strong passive influence of Scorpio rising, Saturn and Mercury in Capricorn and the Venus–Pluto conjunction in Pisces) but in maturity he consciously used his hypnotic qualities to achieve his aims. In his ctress (fifth house)

wife and possibly one
s children, especially his
kind to them (Pisces) but he
trolling and protective (Venus
elt strong urges to escape from
. His children were a great drain
of the fifth, Neptune, situated in his

e sign that it rules – gave Dickens tremendous
usiasm where his work was concerned. Before
l-time writer he was employed in the legal profession
and then as a stenographer and journalist (strong third
d Jupiter in Gemini). Mars in the sixth can produce
olics and Dickens certainly strained his abundant energy
e limits, especially where his writing was concerned, but he
o found time for travel, entertainment and an active social life.
He disliked taking a back-seat in any situation and always projected
the leadership qualities typical of Mars in Aries.

As far as his health was concerned, Mars here had its positive and negative effects. In the physically strong sign of Aries it endowed him with much energy and excellent recuperative powers, but with the continuous pressure of hard work, the powerful square between Mars and Saturn slowly undermined his innately sound constitution and he began to suffer from minor nagging problems which gradually became worse until eventually in his middle fifties he was beset by bad health from which he died at the age of 58.

Seventh House

One of the five empty houses in Dickens' chart. With Taurus on the cusp he was inherently loyal and stable within permanent relationships, but his strong fifth house craved romance, intensity and deep powerful emotions within his marriage (the ruler of the seventh, Venus, situated in the fifth, conjunct Pluto). Unfortunately, he also desired security, passivity and solidity from a partner and was therefore attracted to earthy, mothering Taurean-type women like his wife, who was unable to fulfil his more sensitive, intangible emotional needs. Despite his allegedly unhappy marriage Dickens remained with his wife for twenty-two years (the fixed angles of Scorpio, Taurus, find it extremely difficult to break from a situation), and for much of this time was physically faithful to her. (The ruler of the empty seventh being placed in the fifth is also indicative of the extreme fruitfulness of the marriage.)

EIGHTH HOUSE

Jupiter in Dickens' chart appears to have operated in both the eighth and ninth houses, being placed in the eighth but close to the ninth cusp. From a very early age he was avidly interested in birth and death, and throughout his life was morbidly attracted to morgues and corpses. With the ruler of the eighth, Mercury, being placed in his third, much of this ghoulish interest was transferred to his writing. His mind was highly active and he enjoyed exploring the depths and degradation of humanity. If he had lived in this day and age he would have made a very good psychiatrist (Scorpio rising and Jupiter in the eighth). He developed many spiritual qualities and was a great believer in the after-life, experiencing several visitations and psychically orientated experiences. Physically he was intense, sentimental and passionate (Venus–Pluto) but Jupiter in Gemini was probably more concerned with the mental analysis of his feelings within his marriage rather than anything stronger. Jupiter in the eighth was also responsible for him taking on the debts and burdens of others.

NINTH HOUSE

Although this house is empty, Jupiter, only seven degrees away, certainly had much influence here. Dickens developed a love of travelling and spent a great deal of his time in America and travelling around Europe. He did, however, find it difficult to like or feel at home in many of the places he visited (The Sun, ruler of individuality and ego identity placed in the fourth house of home combined with sensitive, homely Cancer on the cusp of the ninth), and was always pleased to return home. He enjoyed being near water and found Venice a 'marvellous' place (a water sign on the cusp of the ninth, and the strong Pisces influence in the sociable fifth house).

The ninth house can also represent writing, usually on a higher level than the more mundane third house. Dickens could write on both levels and concerned himself with people and situations from all walks of life (the versatility and expansiveness of Jupiter in Gemini). Much of his travelling was undertaken for practical reasons – to write about America and therefore earn money from doing so (the ruler of the ninth in the second house).

TENTH HOUSE

The house of career, aims and ambitions is strangely empty, indicating perhaps that Dickens was not over-ambitious. The prominent second and sixth houses suggest that his main motivators to succeed were his need to be financially secure (second house) and his need to feel usefully occupied within his existence (sixth house). Leo on the cusp of the tenth often gives success, as well as power and respect in one's chosen career. The ruler of the tenth (Sun) situated in the fourth house is usually indicative of a career centred around or operative from the home, and being placed in Aquarius shows his liking for independence both in the home and within his career.

The tenth is also the house of the mother. Dickens was never very close to his mother who was theatrical (Leo on the cusp of the tenth), unstable (Moon in Sagittarius), and undemonstrative (ruler of the tenth in Aquarius). He felt separated and alien from her as a child, and later in life blamed her for much. He never forgot a misdeed or an injury to his character (typical of the retentiveness of Scorpio and the unforgiving nature of Capricorn).

ELEVENTH HOUSE

Dickens had many friends, some very loyal and long-standing, yet his eleventh house is empty, signifying that deep, enduring companionship was not overly important to him. The fact that the ruler Mercury is in the third probably explains his apparent need for friends. He thoroughly enjoyed communicating, especially on a mundane level, and he undoubtedly used the characters of many of his friends within his writing. Some of his relatives and siblings were also close friends (the ruler of the eleventh in the third). He could be very critical, choosy and analytical with friends, and enjoyed variety (Virgo on the cusp of the eleventh).

TWELFTH HOUSE

Another empty house. Libra on the cusp signifies that Dickens found a strange sense of beauty within institutions, particularly hospitals and prisons, the latter of which he became closely associated with and intrigued by as a child, when his father was sent to prison for non-payment of debts. The ruler of the twelfth, Venus, placed in the fifth conjunct Pluto is also a strong indication of his intense, obsessive interest in twelfth house affairs. Venus conjunct Pluto is often indicative of losses in love and Dickens did in fact suffer much trauma and heartbreak through several deaths of females he revered in life.

Note: Within the above interpretation I have often referred to the rulers of the houses, especially where added information regarding the empty houses is required. These rulers are always the rulers of the sign on the cusp of the relevant house. As mentioned in Lesson 8 this system of interpretation is quite complex and can only be utilised effectively with time and patience.

The following questions are mainly based upon information given in the text, but in order to test your overall interpretive abilities I have added a few unmentioned factors which necessitate thorough absorption of the previous lessons.

1. Which second house planet in Dickens' chart is responsible for his strong need for security in his financial status?
2. In which house and sign is the ruler of the seventh house placed?
3. Name the houses and planets mainly attributable to Dickens' writing ability.
4. Which two planets are responsible for Dickens' obsessive love nature?
5. Which house represents his mother, and where is the ruling planet placed?
6. Dickens was a lonely child with many fears and frustrated aims, especially within his education, which was abruptly stopped for a while when he was 12. Name the house and planet which are mainly attributable to these factors.
7. Which is the handle planet of the 'Bucket' shaping?
8. Where should one look to find what type of woman Dickens would seek as a marriage partner? In zodiacal terms, what might she be like?
9. Describe Dickens' outer personality, with reference to the chart.
10. What does a lack of planets in the tenth house generally signify?

Answers

1. Introduction to Signs and Planets

1. ♉ (Taurus)
2. ♑
3. Any of the following words would be suitable: Energy, aggression, assertiveness, sexuality, anger, drive.
4. ♅ ♆ ♇ (Uranus, Neptune and Pluto)
5. ☉ ☽ ☿ ♀ ♂ (Sun, Moon, Mercury, Venus and Mars)
6. If you used any of the following words then you should congratulate yourself: generous, proud, fun-loving, egocentric, stubborn, bombastic, noisy, lazy, showy, theatrical, bossy, unrelenting, likeable, sociable, luxury-loving, sunny-natured.
7. ☿ (Mercury)
8. Any of the following would be applicable: Eccentric, perverse, rebellious, unconventional, unusual, changeable, disruptive, stimulating, exciting, inventive.
9. ♃ (Jupiter)
10. ♐ (Sagittarius)

2. Sign Groupings and Intepretations

1. ♉ ♋ ♍ ♏ ♑ ♓
   (Taurus, Cancer, Virgo, Scorpio, Capricorn, Pisces.)
2. Masculine/Feminine, Negative/Positive.
3. Air.
4. ♈ ♌ ♐ (Aries, Leo, Sagittarius).
5. Any of the following would be appropriate: self-seeking, self-centred or self-orientated, drive, push, ardour, enthusiasm, assertiveness.
6. A typical answer would be as follows: A Taurus person represents his fixity of character through his attitude towards materialistic issues. This sign enjoys the luxuries of life and usually holds on to its financial accumulations and worldly posssessions.
   (If you answered this question in a similar manner, or added any typical Taurean qualities, then you are entitled to consider yourself correct.)
7. ♐ (Sagittarius).

8. Any of the following would be suitable:
Emotions, sensitivity, intuition, kindness, caring, grasping, dreamy, artistic ability, sacrificial, spiritual, destructive, lax morals, controlling, protective, supportive, sympathetic.
(If you gave four or more words for your answer, then you can congratulate yourself. A one word answer, however, should necessitate reading the text again.)
9. ♏ (Scorpio). It is a Water sign and the other three are Earth signs.
10. ♎ (Libra). Active, Cardinal, Air.

This questionnaire was slightly more difficult than that of Lesson 1. Do not be discouraged if you found the interpretation questions difficult. At this stage single-syllable answers are quite satisfactory, and if you scored seven or more correct answers in this manner, then you should feel able to move on to Lesson 3.

3. BIRTH CHART CALCULATION

1. No. (21 March was the changeover date for this year.)
2. 6 Minutes 08 Seconds.
3. Deduct 24 hours to make a usable local sidereal time of 6 08 21.
4. Minus 80 seconds (1 minute 20 seconds)
5. 7 16 01
6. Asc. 16 degrees Sagittarius, MC 19 degrees Libra.
7. 21 44 05
8. 4 20 40 (sidereal time). MC 7 degrees Gemini
9. 23 14 10
10. ASC.29 degrees Capricorn. MC 3 degrees Sagittarius

4. BIRTH CHART ERECTION

1. Count UPWARDS.
2. 4 degrees Taurus. (♉)
3. 1 degree 4 minutes.
4. ℞ = Retrograde, D = Direct.
5. 24 January.
6. 3 degrees Aries. ♈
7. 27 July.
8. 24 hours (one day).

9.	Mercury		(☿)
10.	Active	7	(☉ ☽ ☿ ♂ ♄ ♆ ♇)
	Passive	3	(♀ ♃ ♅)
	Fire	6	(☉ ☽ ♀ ♂ ♄ ♆)
	Earth	2	(♀ ♃)
	Air	1	(♇)
	Water	1	(♅)
	Cardinal	3	(☽ ♀ ♇)
	Fixed	3	(♃ ♄ ♅)
	Mutable	4	(☉ ☿ ♂ ♆)

5. Calculation of Aspects

1. The square □
2. A conjunction ☌
3. ☌ ⚺ ✱ □ △ ⚻ ☍
4. No.
5. A Quincunx ⚻
6. Yes.
7. A sextile ✱
8. 4 degrees.
9. Five
10. (a) □ (b) ✱ (c) △
    (d) ☌ (e) ⚺ (f) ⚻
    (g) ☍

6. Interpretation: Planets in Signs

Note: In the answers which tell you to refer to text, similar descriptive words are allowed. Use your own judgement as to their accuracy. A minimum of two-word answers are acceptable.

1. Refer to text in Lesson 6.
2. No. Libra is a mental sign in which Mars is in detriment (Lesson 8 describes this term).
3. Refer to text in Lesson 6.
4. Ego, individuality, inner self, etc.
5. Refer to text in Lesson 6.
6. The water signs, Cancer, Scorpio and Pisces.
7. The Moon represents our emotions, habits, feelings, responses, life-patterns, etc.
8. Taurus or Capricorn.

9. The houses.
10. Burdens, responsibilities, limitations, fears, coldness. It also teaches us valuable lessons in life.

7. INTERPRETATION: PLANETS IN HOUSES

Note: In the answers which tell you to refer to the text, similar descriptive words are allowed. Use your own judgement as to their accuracy. A minimum of two-word answers are acceptable.

1. Angular, succedent and cadent.
2. 5th.
3. Refer to text in Lesson 7.
4. Refer to text in Lesson 7.
5. 11th.
6. 4th and 10th.
7. The 7th.
8. Friendships, and group and social activities.
9. Refer to text in Lesson 7.
10. Refer to text in Lesson 7.

8. INTERPRETATION: OTHER CONFIGURATIONS

1. ♂
2. ♄ ♃ ☿ ☉
3. Yes. Two. Uranus in Diagram 14 (Example Chart No. 4); and Mercury in Diagram 15 (Example Chart No. 5).
4. A stellium.
5. ♄ in Libra, ♂ in Capricorn.
6. Refer to text in Lesson 8.
7. Refer to text in Lesson 8.
8. ♑
9. ☿ ♀ ♂
10. At 15 degrees Leo in the third house.

9. PREDICTIVE ASTROLOGY

Note: The replies to questions 7 and 10 are variable. Refer to the text and use your own judgement as to the accuracy of your response.

1. The personal planets ☉ ☽ ☿ ♀ ♂
2. Fifty-two.
3. Approximately thirty years.
4. ☽ Approximately 12 degrees.

5. The five outermost planets ♃ ♄ ♅ ♆ ♇
6. Aged 28 to 30 (approx.)
7. Sudden or unexpected change of career, aims or ambitions, or erratic unusual events occurring within the career environment.
8. ♂
9. Approximately once every twelve years.
10. Become less communicative and lively generally (☿ leaving the third house) but more interested in communicating and relating ideas on all home and emotional affairs.

10. SAMPLE ANALYSIS: CHARLES DICKENS

1. ☽
2. In ♓ in the fifth house.
3. Third and ninth houses: ☿ and ♃
4. ♀ and ♇
5. The tenth. Ruling planet ☉ in the fourth.
6. ♄ In Capricorn in the third house.
7. ♃
8. The seventh house cusp – which is ♉ , denoting a loyal, dependable, earthy and motherly type.
9. Refer to text.
10. Lack of, or easy acceptance of, ambition and aims in life.

APPENDICES

APPENDIX 1: BRITISH SUMMERTIME 1916 TO 1992

	Commenced	*Ended*		*Commenced*	*Ended*
1916	21 May	1 Oct.	1957	14 Apr.	6 Oct.
1917	8 Apr.	17 Sept.	1958	20 Apr.	5 Oct.
1918	24 Mar.	30 Sept.	1959	19 Apr.	4 Oct.
1919	30 Mar.	29 Sept.	1960	10 Apr.	2 Oct.
1920	28 Mar.	25 Oct.	1961	26 Mar.	29 Oct.
1921	3 Apr.	3 Oct.	1962	25 Mar.	28 Oct.
1922	26 Mar.	8 Oct.	1963	31 Mar.	27 Oct.
1923	22 Apr.	16 Sept.	1964	22 Mar.	25 Oct.
1924	20 Apr.	21 Sept.	1965	21 Mar.	24 Oct.
1925 to	3rd Sun. in	1 Sun. in	1966	20 Mar.	23 Oct.
1938 incl.	Apr.	Oct.	1967	19 Mar.	29 Oct.
1939	16 Apr.	19 Nov.	1968 to	18 Feb.	continued
1940	25 Feb.	Continued	1970 incl.	Continued with British Summertime	
1941–4 incl. Continuation of British Summertime throughout these years, plus the addition of Double Summertime.			1971	Continued	31 Oct.
			1972	19 Mar.	29 Oct.
			1973	18 Mar.	28 Oct.
			1974	17 Mar.	27 Oct.
1941	4 May	10 Aug.	1975	16 Mar.	26 Oct.
1942	5 Apr.	9 Aug.	1976	21 Mar.	24 Oct.
1943	4 Apr.	15 Aug.	1977	20 Mar.	23 Oct.
1944	2 Apr.	17 Sept.	1978	19 Mar.	29 Oct.
1945	2 Apr.	15 July	1979	18 Mar.	28 Oct.
1945	Continued	7 Oct.	1980	16 Mar.	26 Oct.
1946	14 Apr.	6 Oct.	1981	29 Mar.	25 Oct.
1947	16 Mar.	2 Nov.	1982	28 Mar.	24 Oct.
plus Double Summertime between			1983	27 Mar.	23 Oct.
1947	13 Apr.	10 Aug.	1984	25 Mar.	28 Oct.
1948	14 Mar.	31 Oct.	1985	31 Mar.	27 Oct.
1949	3 Apr.	30 Oct.	1986	30 Mar.	26 Oct.
1950	16 Apr.	22 Oct.	1987	29 Mar.	25 Oct.
1951	15 Apr.	21 Oct.	1988	27 Mar.	23 Oct.
1952	20 Apr.	26 Oct.	1989	26 Mar.	29 Oct.
1953	19 Apr.	4 Oct.	1989	26 Mar.	29 Oct.
1954	11 Apr.	3 Oct.	1990	25 Mar.	28 Oct.
1955	17 Apr.	2 Oct.	1991	31 Mar.	27 Oct.
1956	15 Apr.	7 Oct.	1992	29 Mar.	25 Oct.

Note: All times change at 2.00 a.m. GMT.

Appendix 2:
Positions of Pluto

1941				**1963**				**1970**			
1/1	3	40	R	1/1	12	04	R	1/1	27	23	R
1/2	2	59	R	9/1	11	59	R	7/2	26	58	R
15/4	2	01	DD	25/2	10	59	R	19/3	25	59	R
24/6	3	01	D	7/4	9	59	R	30/4	24	59	R
30/7	4	00	D	24/5	9	32	DD	6/6	24	40	DD
6/9	5	00	D	4/7	10	01	D	10/7	25	00	D
7/11	5	47	RR	9/8	11	00	D	17/8	26	00	D
31/12	5	10	R	8/9	12	01	D	14/9	27	00	D
				7/10	13	00	D	12/10	28	02	D
				18/11	14	00	D	12/11	29	00	D
				18/12	14	13	RR	31/12	29	42	D
				31/12	14	10	R				

Key
R = Retrograde
D = Direct
RR = Turned Retrograde on given date
DD = Turned Direct on given date

Appendix 3:
Astrological Book and Stationery Suppliers

Astrological stationery, chart forms and ephemerids are available from the following suppliers:

W.Foulsham & Co. Ltd, Yeovil Road, Slough, Berks SL1 4JH. Tel: 0753 26769 (ephemerides for all years)

L. N. Fowler & Co. Ltd, 1201, High Road, Chadwell Heath, Romford, Essex RM6 4DH

Compendium Bookshop, 234 Camden High Street, London NW1.

Mysteries, 9 Monmouth Street, London WC2.

W. & G. Foyle Limited, 119 Charing Cross Road, London WC2.
Watkins Books Limited, 21 Cecil Court, London WC2.

Appendix 4:
Raphael's Astronomical Ephemeris (Excerpts)

Reproduced by kind permission of the copyright holders, W. Foulsham & Company Ltd.

See the tables on pages 124 to 131

Appendix 5:
Tables of Houses

Reproduced by kind permission of the copyright holders, W. Foulsham & Company Ltd.

See the tables on pages 132 to 137

New Moon—July 24, 7*h.* 38*m.* 40*s. a.m.*

D M	Neptune. Lat.	Neptune. Dec.	Herschel. Lat.	Herschel. Dec.	Saturn. Lat.	Saturn. Dec.	Jupiter. Lat.	Jupiter. Dec.	Mars. Lat.	Mars. Declin.	
	° ′	° ′	° ′	° ′	° ′	° ′	° ′	° ′	° ′	° ′	° ′
1	1N16	3N 7	0S13	19N39	2S 4	16N53	0S41	21N 0	3S14	3S 8	2S55
3	1 16	3 6	0 13	19 40	2 4	16 56	0 41	21 4	3 17	2 43	2 31
5	1 16	3 5	0 13	19 41	2 4	16 59	0 41	21 8	3 20	2 19	2 7
7	1 16	3 4	0 13	19 43	2 4	17 1	0 41	21 12	3 23	1 55	1 43
9	1 16	3 4	0 13	19 44	2 5	17 4	0 41	21 16	3 27	1 31	1 20
11	1 16	3 3	0 13	19 45	2 5	17 6	0 41	21 20	3 30	1 8	0 57
13	1 15	3 2	0 13	19 46	2 5	17 9	0 41	21 23	3 33	0 45	0 34
15	1 15	3 1	0 13	19 47	2 5	17 11	0 41	21 27	3 36	0 23	0 12
17	1 15	3 0	0 13	19 48	2 6	17 13	0 41	21 30	3 39	0 2	0N 9
19	1 15	2 59	0 13	19 49	2 6	17 15	0 41	21 33	3 42	0N19	0 30
21	1 15	2 57	0 13	19 50	2 6	17 17	0 41	21 36	3 45	0 40	0 50
23	1 15	2 56	0 13	19 51	2 6	17 19	0 41	21 39	3 48	1 0	1 9
25	1 15	2 55	0 13	19 52	2 7	17 21	0 41	21 42	3 51	1 19	1 28
27	1 15	2 54	0 13	19 52	2 7	17 23	0 41	21 45	3 54	1 38	1 47
29	1 15	2 53	0 13	19 53	2 7	17 24	0 41	21 48	3 57	1 56	2 4
31	1 15	2 51	0 13	19 54	2 8	17 26	0 41	21 50	4 0	2 13	

D M	D W	Sidereal Time.	☉ Long.	☉ Dec.	☽ Long.	☽ Lat.	☽ Dec.	MIDNIGHT. ☽ Long.	MIDNIGHT. ☽ Dec.
		H. M. S.	° ′ ″	° ′	° ′ ″	° ′	° ′	° ′ ″	° ′
1	Tu	6 36 35	9♋14 20	23N 7	0♎24 46	0N24	0N12	7♎20 11	1S59
2	W	6 40 32	10 11 32	23 3	14 19 18	1 36	4S10	21 22 7	6 19
3	Th	6 44 29	11 8 44	22 59	28 28 34	2 44	8 23	5♏38 29	10 21
4	F	6 48 25	12 5 56	22 54	12♏51 34	3 42	12 10	20 7 26	13 49
5	S	6 52 22	13 3 7	22 48	27 25 30	4 26	15 16	4♐45 8	16 28
6	𝔖	6 56 18	14 0 18	22 43	12♐ 5 31	4 54	17 23	19 25 48	18 2
7	M	7 0 15	14 57 29	22 36	26 45 2	5 2	18 22	4♑ 2 16	18 24
8	Tu	7 4 11	15 54 40	22 30	11♑16 35	4 51	18 8	18 27 6	17 35
9	W	7 8 8	16 51 51	22 23	25 33 4	4 21	16 45	2♒33 49	15 41
10	Th	7 12 5	17 49 2	22 16	9♒28 51	3 37	14 24	16 17 51	12 56
11	F	7 16 1	18 46 13	22 8	23 0 38	2 41	11 19	29 37 9	9 35
12	S	7 19 58	19 43 25	22 0	6♓ 7 33	1 38	7 45	12♓32 3	5 51
13	𝔖	7 23 54	20 40 38	21 51	18 51 2	0 32	3 56	25 4 56	1 59
14	M	7 27 51	21 37 51	21 42	1♈14 18	0S34	0 2	7♈19 41	1N53
15	Tu	7 31 47	22 35 4	21 33	13 21 43	1 38	3N47	19 21 3	5 37
16	W	7 35 44	23 32 18	21 24	25 18 20	2 36	7 22	1♉14 15	9 4
17	Th	7 39 40	24 29 33	21 14	7♉ 9 25	3 26	10 39	13 4 31	12 8
18	F	7 43 37	25 26 49	21 3	19 0 7	4 8	13 29	24 56 48	14 43
19	S	7 47 33	26 24 5	20 53	0♊55 6	4 40	15 47	6♊55 30	16 41
20	𝔖	7 51 30	27 21 22	20 42	12 58 25	4 59	17 25	19 4 13	17 57
21	M	7 55 27	28 18 39	20 30	25 13 13	5 5	18 17	1♋25 37	18 23
22	Tu	7 59 23	29 15 57	20 19	7♋41 37	4 57	18 17	14 1 17	17 57
23	W	8 3 20	0♌13 16	20 6	20 24 40	4 34	17 23	26 51 44	16 35
24	Th	8 7 16	1 10 36	19 54	3♌22 23	3 57	15 34	9♌56 32	14 20
25	F	8 11 13	2 7 56	19 41	16 33 59	3 6	12 55	23 14 35	11 19
26	S	8 15 9	3 5 17	19 28	29 58 7	2 4	9 33	6♍44 26	7 39
27	𝔖	8 19 6	4 2 38	19 15	13♍33 20	0 54	5 38	20 24 39	3 32
28	M	8 23 2	5 0 0	19 1	27 18 14	0N20	1 22	4♎13 58	0S49
29	Tu	8 26 59	5 57 23	18 47	11♎11 44	1 33	3S 0	18 11 24	5 9
30	W	8 30 56	6 54 46	18 33	25 12 53	2 42	7 15	2♏16 2	9 14
31	Th	8 34 52	7 52 9	18 18	9♏20 44	3 41	11 7	16 26 47	12 49

First Quarter—July 2, 4*h.* 23*m.* 59*s. a.m.*; July 31, 9*h.* 19*m.* 10*s. a.m.*

Full Moon—July 8, 8*h*. 17*m*. 20*s*. *p.m.*

D M	Venus Lat. ° ′	Venus Declin. ° ′	Venus Declin. ° ′	Mercury Lat. ° ′	Mercury Declin. ° ′	Mercury Declin. ° ′	☽ Node. ° ′
1	1 N 27	21 N 50	21 N 36	4 S 20	18 N 39	18 N 33	26 ♍ 34
3	1 29	21 21	21 5	4 36	18 28	18 25	26 27
5	1 31	20 49	20 32	4 44	18 23	18 22	26 21
7	1 32	20 15	19 57	4 50	18 23	18 25	26 15
9	1 33	19 38	19 20	4 47	18 28	18 33	26 8
11	1 34	19 0	18 40	4 39	18 38	18 45	26 2
13	1 35	18 20	17 59	4 25	18 53	19 2	25 56
15	1 36	17 37	17 15	4 7	19 11	19 21	25 49
17	1 36	16 53	16 30	3 45	19 32	19 43	25 43
19	1 35	16 7	15 43	3 20	19 54	20 5	25 36
21	1 35	15 19	14 54	2 52	20 17	20 28	25 30
23	1 34	14 29	14 4	2 24	20 39	20 49	25 24
25	1 33	13 38	13 12	1 54	20 58	21 7	25 17
27	1 32	12 46	12 19	1 25	21 14	21 20	25 11
29	1 30	11 52	11 25	0 56	21 25	21 28	25 5
31	1 28	10 58		0 28	21 29		24 58

Mutual Aspects.

1. ☉∠♄. ♀✱♅. ♂P♆.
2. ☉☌☿. ♀△♂.
4. ☿∠♄. ♀P♃.
5. ☉Q♆. ☿⊻♃. ♀☌♇.
6. ☉∠♅.
8. ☉⊥♃. ☿⊻♀. ♀Q♄. ♂△♇. ♄△♆.
9. ♀P♅.
10. ♀✱♃, ∠♆. 11. ♀Q♅.
12. ☿⊥ & P♀.
13. ☿□♂.
16. ☉P♃. ♀P♄.
18. ☉✱♆. ♀⊥♆.
19. ☉✱♄. ☿P♅.
20. ☉∠♃.
22. ☉P☿, ✱♅. ♀Q♃.
23. ☿∠♀. ♀⊻♆. ♂∠♄.
24. ☉P♅. ☿∠♄. ♀⚼♂, □♄.
25. ☿□♂.
26. ☿⊻♃, Q♆. ♀□♅.
27. ☉☌♇. ☿∠♅.
28. ♂✱♃. 30. ♀⊻♇.
31. ☿∠♀, ⊥♃. ♂∠♅.

D M	♆ Long. ° ′	♅ Long. ° ′	♄ Long. ° ′	♃ Long. ° ′	♂ Long. ° ′	♀ Long. ° ′	☿ Long. ° ′	☉	♇	♆	♅	♄	♃	♂	♀	☿
1	25 ♍ 5	28 ♉ 39	24 ♉ 28	8 ♊ 13	29 ♓ 35	28 ♋ 46	11 ♋ 24		✱	☌	△	△		☍	✱	
2	25 6	28 42	24 34	8 26	0 ♈ 10	29 59	10 ℞ 47	□			⚼	⚼	△			□
3	25 7	28 45	24 40	8 39	0 45	1 ♌ 12	10 11		□	⊻			⚼		□	
4	25 8	28 47	24 46	8 52	1 19	2 25	9 35	△		∠				⚼		△
5	25 9	28 50	24 52	9 5	1 53	3 39	9 1	⚼	△	✱	☍	☍		△	△	⚼
S	25 10	28 53	24 58	9 18	2 27	4 52	8 28		⚼				☍			
7	25 11	28 55	25 4	9 30	3 1	6 5	7 58			□				□	⚼	
8	25 12	28 58	25 10	9 43	3 34	7 18	7 31	☍			⚼	⚼				☍
9	25 13	29 1	25 16	9 56	4 8	8 31	7 8			△	△	△	⚼			
10	25 14	29 3	25 21	10 8	4 41	9 44	6 49		☍	⚼			△	✱	☍	
11	25 15	29 6	25 27	10 21	5 13	10 57	6 34				□	□		∠		⚼
12	25 16	29 8	25 33	10 33	5 46	12 10	6 23	⚼					□	⊻		△
S	25 17	29 11	25 38	10 45	6 18	13 23	6 18	△	⚼							
14	25 18	29 13	25 44	10 58	6 50	14 36	6 D 18		△	☍	✱	✱		☌	⚼	□
15	25 20	29 16	25 49	11 10	7 21	15 50	6 23				∠	∠	✱		△	
16	25 21	29 18	25 54	11 22	7 53	17 3	6 33	□			⊻	⊻	∠			
17	25 22	29 20	26 0	11 34	8 24	18 16	6 49		□	⚼			⊻	⊻		✱
18	25 23	29 23	26 5	11 46	8 54	19 28	7 11							∠	□	∠
19	25 25	29 25	26 10	11 58	9 25	20 41	7 38	✱	✱	△	☌	☌				
S	25 26	29 27	26 15	12 10	9 55	21 54	8 11	∠	∠				☌	✱		⊻
21	25 28	29 29	26 20	12 22	10 24	23 7	8 50	⊻		□	⊻	⊻			✱	
22	25 29	29 31	26 25	12 33	10 53	24 20	9 34		⊻			∠	⊻	□	∠	☌
23	25 30	29 33	26 30	12 45	11 22	25 33	10 23			✱	∠	✱			⊻	
24	25 32	29 36	26 34	12 56	11 51	26 46	11 18	☌	☌		✱		∠			
25	25 33	29 38	26 39	13 8	12 19	27 59	12 18			∠			✱	△		⊻
26	25 35	29 40	26 44	13 19	12 47	29 12	13 24	⊻	⊻	⊻	□	□		⚼	☌	∠
S	25 36	29 41	26 48	13 30	13 14	0 ♍ 24	14 34	∠	∠				□			✱
28	25 38	29 43	26 52	13 42	13 41	1 37	15 50		✱	●	△	△			⊻	
29	25 39	29 45	26 57	13 53	14 7	2 50	17 11	✱			⚼	⚼	△	☍		□
30	25 41	29 47	27 1	14 4	14 33	4 3	18 36			⊻			⚼		∠	
31	25 43	29 49	27 5	14 15	14 59	5 15	20 6	□	□	∠					✱	

(The nine symbol columns on the right are headed **Lunar Aspects.**)

Last Quarter—July 16, 8*h*. 7*m*. 19*s*. *a.m.*

New Moon—October 17, 0h. 43m. p.m.

D M	Neptune Lat.	Neptune Dec.	Herschel Lat.	Herschel Dec.	Saturn Lat.	Saturn Dec.	Jupiter Lat.	Jupiter Dec.	Mars Lat.	Mars Dec.	
	° ′	° ′	° ′	° ′	° ′	° ′	° ′	° ′	° ′	° ′	° ′
1	1 N43	14 S 25	0 N44	9 N23	1 S 15	17 S 0	1 S 38	4 N33	0 S 21	16 S 4	16 S 17
3	1 43	14 26	0 44	9 20	1 15	17 1	1 38	4 27	0 22	16 30	16 43
5	1 43	14 27	0 44	9 18	1 15	17 2	1 38	4 21	0 24	16 56	17 8
7	1 43	14 28	0 44	9 15	1 15	17 3	1 38	4 14	0 25	17 21	17 33
9	1 43	14 29	0 44	9 13	1 15	17 4	1 38	4 8	0 26	17 45	17 57
11	1 43	14 31	0 44	9 11	1 15	17 4	1 38	4 2	0 27	18 9	18 21
13	1 43	14 32	0 44	9 8	1 15	17 5	1 38	3 56	0 29	18 33	18 45
15	1 43	14 33	0 44	9 6	1 14	17 5	1 38	3 50	0 30	18 56	19 7
17	1 43	14 35	0 44	9 4	1 14	17 5	1 37	3 44	0 31	19 18	19 29
19	1 43	14 36	0 44	9 2	1 14	17 5	1 37	3 38	0 32	19 40	19 51
21	1 43	14 37	0 44	9 0	1 14	17 5	1 37	3 32	0 33	20 1	20 12
23	1 43	14 38	0 44	8 58	1 14	17 5	1 37	3 27	0 34	20 22	20 32
25	1 43	14 40	0 45	8 56	1 14	17 5	1 36	3 21	0 35	20 42	20 51
27	1 43	14 41	0 45	8 54	1 14	17 5	1 36	3 16	0 36	21 1	21 10
29	1 43	14 42	0 45	8 52	1 14	17 4	1 36	3 11	0 38	21 19	21 28
31	1 43	14 44	0 45	8 51	1 14	17 3	1 35	3 6	0 39	21 37	

D M	D W	Sidereal Time	☉ Long.	☉ Dec.	☽ Long.	☽ Lat.	☽ Dec.	MIDNIGHT ☽ Long.	MIDNIGHT ☽ Dec.
		H. M. S.	° ′ ″	° ′	° ′ ″	° ′	° ′	° ′ ″	° ′
1	Tu	12 38 0	7 ♎ 35 11	3 S 1	14 ♓ 17 48	4 S 14	10 S 5	21 ♓ 32 42	7 S 31
2	W	12 41 56	8 34 10	3 24	28 53 13	4 46	4 49	6 ♈ 18 24	2 1
3	Th	12 45 53	9 33 12	3 47	13 ♈ 47 13	5 0	0 N 50	21 18 26	3 N 41
4	F	12 49 49	10 32 15	4 10	28 50 47	4 53	6 29	6 ♉ 23 1	9 12
5	S	12 53 46	11 31 21	4 34	13 ♉ 53 52	4 26	11 46	21 22 14	14 9
6	𝕾	12 57 43	12 30 29	4 57	28 47 8	3 42	16 17	6 ♊ 7 46	18 9
7	M	13 1 39	13 29 39	5 20	13 ♊ 23 31	2 43	19 43	20 33 59	20 57
8	Tu	13 5 36	14 28 51	5 43	27 38 55	1 35	21 50	4 ♋ 38 15	22 22
9	W	13 9 32	15 28 6	6 5	11 ♋ 32 2	0 23	22 33	18 20 27	22 24
10	Th	13 13 29	16 27 24	6 28	25 3 45	0 N 48	21 55	1 ♌ 42 13	21 7
11	F	13 17 25	17 26 43	6 51	8 ♌ 16 14	1 55	20 3	14 46 7	18 44
12	S	13 21 22	18 26 5	7 14	21 12 13	2 54	17 11	27 34 53	15 27
13	𝕾	13 25 18	19 25 29	7 36	3 ♍ 54 25	3 44	13 33	10 ♍ 11 5	11 31
14	M	13 29 15	20 24 56	7 59	16 25 6	4 22	9 23	22 36 43	7 10
15	Tu	13 33 12	21 24 24	8 21	28 46 4	4 47	4 53	4 ♎ 53 18	2 34
16	W	13 37 8	22 23 55	8 43	10 ♎ 58 34	4 59	0 14	17 1 58	2 S 5
17	Th	13 41 5	23 23 28	9 5	23 3 36	4 57	4 S 22	29 3 37	6 36
18	F	13 45 1	24 23 2	9 27	5 ♏ 2 7	4 42	8 47	10 ♏ 59 17	10 51
19	S	13 48 58	25 22 39	9 49	16 55 18	4 14	12 50	22 50 23	14 41
20	𝕾	13 52 54	26 22 18	10 11	28 44 48	3 36	16 23	4 ♐ 38 54	17 55
21	M	13 56 51	27 21 58	10 32	10 ♐ 33 1	2 48	19 16	16 27 34	20 25
22	Tu	14 0 47	28 21 41	10 54	22 23 2	1 53	21 21	28 19 56	22 3
23	W	14 4 44	29 21 25	11 15	4 ♑ 18 49	0 52	22 30	10 ♑ 20 17	22 42
24	Th	14 8 41	0 ♏ 21 11	11 36	16 24 58	0 S 12	22 38	22 33 30	22 17
25	F	14 12 37	1 20 59	11 57	28 46 34	1 17	21 40	5 ♒ 4 48	20 46
26	S	14 16 34	2 20 48	12 17	11 ♒ 28 50	2 20	19 35	17 59 16	18 8
27	𝕾	14 20 30	3 20 39	12 38	24 36 34	3 18	16 25	1 ♓ 21 11	14 28
28	M	14 24 27	4 20 32	12 58	8 ♓ 13 21	4 6	12 17	15 13 12	9 55
29	Tu	14 28 23	5 20 26	13 18	22 20 38	4 42	7 21	29 35 21	4 39
30	W	14 32 20	6 20 22	13 38	6 ♈ 56 48	5 1	1 51	14 ♈ 24 13	1 N 1
31	Th	14 36 16	7 20 20	13 58	21 56 36	5 0	3 N 55	29 32 45	6 46

First Quarter—October 25, 5h. 21m. p.m.

FULL MOON—October 3, 4*h*. 44*m*. *a.m.*

D M	Venus Lat. ° ′	Venus Declin. ° ′	Venus Declin. ° ′	Mercury Lat. ° ′	Mercury Declin. ° ′	Mercury Declin. ° ′	☽ Node. ° ′
1	1N 4	5 S 25	5 S 55	0N 29	4 N 2	4 N 5	16♒12
3	1 1	6 25	6 55	0 57	4 3	3 56	16 6
5	0 58	7 25	7 54	1 20	3 45	3 29	16 0
7	0 54	8 23	8 53	1 37	3 10	2 46	15 53
9	0 50	9 22	9 50	1 49	2 20	1 50	15 47
11	0 46	10 19	10 47	1 56	1 18	0 44	15 41
13	0 42	11 15	11 43	1 59	0 8	0 S 30	15 34
15	0 38	12 10	12 37	1 58	1 S 9	1 50	15 28
17	0 34	13 4	13 31	1 55	2 31	3 13	15 21
19	0 29	13 57	14 23	1 49	3 55	4 38	15 15
21	0 24	14 49	15 14	1 41	5 21	6 4	15 9
23	0 20	15 39	16 3	1 31	6 47	7 30	15 2
25	0 15	16 27	16 51	1 21	8 12	8 54	14 56
27	0 10	17 14	17 37	1 9	9 36	10 18	14 50
29	0 5	17 59	18 21	0 57	10 59	11 39	14 43
31	0 0	18 42		0 44	12 19		14 37

Mutual Aspects.

1. ⊙⚺♅, ⊥♆. ♀△♄.
3. ♀⊥♇. ♂☌♆. [♂✱♇.
4. ⊙P☿. ☿±♄. ♂∇♃.
5. ⊙P♃.
6. ⊙⚺♇. ♀∠♅. ♂□♄,
8. ⊙☍♃, ⊥♅, ⚺♆. [P♄.
9. ♀P♅. ♃∇♆.
10. ⊙△♄. ☿∠♆. ♀∠♇. ♃±♅.
11. ☿⚼♄. ♂±♃. ♂Q♅.
13. ⊙⊥♇. 15. ☿∠♂. ♂P♇.
16. ☿⚺♅, ⊥♆.
17. ⊙∠♅, P♅. ♃∇♇.
18. ☿☍♃, ⚺♇.
19. ☿P♃, ⊥♅, ⚺♆. ♀✱♅.
20. ⊙⚺♂. ☿△♄. [♂Q♇.
21. ♀P♆. ♄Stat.
22. ⊙∠♇. ☿⊥♇. ♀∇♃. ♂⚼♃.
23. ♀✱♇. 24. ☿⊥♂. ♀☌♆.
25. ☿∠♅. ♀□♄.
26. ☿P♅. ♀±♃.
27. ☿∠♇. ♀P♄.
29. ♀Q♅. 31. ☿⚺♂. ♀P♇.

D M	♆ Long. ° ′	♅ Long. ° ′	♄ Long. ° ′	♃ Long. ° ′	♂ Long. ° ′	♀ Long. ° ′	☿ Long. ° ′	Lunar Aspects ⊙	♇	♆	♅	♄	♃	♂	♀	☿
1	14♏ 3	7♍40	16♒47	15♈22	12♏58	16♎19	20♍57		☍	△	☍	⚺	⚺	△		☍
2	14 5	7 43	16 ℞45	15 ℞14	13 39	17 34	21 24			⚼		∠		⚼		
3	14 7	7 46	16 43	15 6	14 21	18 48	22 0	☍				✱	☌		☍	
4	14 9	7 50	16 42	14 58	15 2	20 3	22 45		⚼		⚼					
5	14 11	7 53	16 40	14 50	15 44	21 18	23 38		△	☍	△	□	⚺	☍		⚼
S	14 13	7 56	16 38	14 42	16 26	22 33	24 39	⚼					∠			△
7	14 15	7 59	16 37	14 34	17 7	23 47	25 47	△	□		□	△	✱		⚼	
8	14 17	8 3	16 36	14 26	17 49	25 2	27 1			⚼		⚼		⚼	△	□
9	14 19	8 6	16 34	14 18	18 31	26 17	28 20	□	✱	△	✱		□			
10	14 21	8 9	16 33	14 10	19 13	27 32	29 44		∠		∠			△	□	✱
11	14 23	8 12	16 32	14 2	19 55	28 46	1♎11		⚺	□	⚺		△			
12	14 25	8 15	16 31	13 54	20 37	0♏ 1	2 42	✱				☍		□		∠
S	14 27	8 18	16 30	13 46	21 19	1 16	4 16	∠			☌		⚼		✱	⚺
14	14 29	8 21	16 29	13 38	22 2	2 31	5 52	⚺	☌	✱				✱	∠	
15	14 31	8 24	16 29	13 30	22 44	3 46	7 29			∠		⚼			⚺	
16	14 33	8 27	16 28	13 22	23 26	5 0	9 8		⚺	⚺	⚺	△	☍	∠		☌
17	14 35	8 30	16 28	13 14	24 9	6 15	10 49	☌	∠		∠			⚺		
18	14 37	8 33	16 27	13 6	24 51	7 30	12 30				✱				☌	
19	14 40	8 36	16 27	12 58	25 34	8 45	14 12		✱	☌		□				⚺
S	14 42	8 39	16 27	12 51	26 16	10 0	15 54	⚺					⚼	☌		∠
21	14 44	8 42	16 27	12 43	26 59	11 14	17 36	∠	□	⚺	□	✱	△		⚺	
22	14 46	8 44	16 D27	12 36	27 42	12 29	19 18							⚺	∠	✱
23	14 48	8 47	16 27	12 28	28 25	13 44	21 0	✱		∠	△	∠				
24	14 50	8 50	16 27	12 21	29 8	14 59	22 42		△	✱		⚺	□	∠	✱	
25	14 53	8 52	16 28	12 14	29 51	16 14	24 24	□	⚼		⚼			✱		□
26	14 55	8 55	16 28	12 7	0♐34	17 28	26 6			□		☌	✱			
S	14 57	8 58	16 29	12 0	1 17	18 43	27 47						∠		□	△
28	14 59	9 0	16 29	11 53	2 0	19 58	29 28	△	☍	△	☍		⚺	□		
29	15 1	9 3	16 30	11 46	2 43	21 13	1♏ 8	⚼				⚺			△	⚼
30	15 4	9 5	16 31	11 39	3 27	22 28	2 48			⚼		∠	☌	△	⚼	
31	15 6	9 8	16 32	11 33	4 10	23 42	4 27		⚼		⚼	✱		⚼		

LAST QUARTER—October 9, 7*h*. 28*m*. *p.m.*

New Moon—January 7*d*, 8*h*. 36*m*. *p.m.*

D M	Neptune Lat.	Neptune Dec.	Herschel Lat.	Herschel Dec.	Saturn Lat.	Saturn Dec.	Jupiter Lat.	Jupiter Dec.	Mars Lat.	Mars Dec.	Mars Dec.
	° ′	° ′	° ′	° ′	° ′	° ′	° ′	° ′	° ′	° ′	° ′
1	1N 39	18 S 31	0N 43	2 S 48	2 S 31	9 N49	1N 13	11 S 10	0 S 48	7 S 34	7 S 16
3	1 39	18 32	0 43	2 48	2 31	9 50	1 13	11 15	0 46	6 58	6 40
5	1 39	18 33	0 43	2 49	2 30	9 50	1 13	11 20	0 44	6 21	6 3
7	1 39	18 33	0 43	2 49	2 30	9 51	1 14	11 25	0 42	5 45	5 26
9	1 39	18 34	0 44	2 49	2 29	9 52	1 14	11 30	0 40	5 8	4 49
11	1 40	18 34	0 44	2 49	2 28	9 53	1 14	11 34	0 37	4 31	4 12
13	1 40	18 35	0 44	2 49	2 28	9 54	1 15	11 38	0 35	3 54	3 35
15	1 40	18 36	0 44	2 49	2 27	9 56	1 15	11 42	0 33	3 16	2 58
17	1 40	18 36	0 44	2 49	2 27	9 57	1 16	11 46	0 31	2 39	2 20
19	1 40	18 37	0 44	2 48	2 26	9 59	1 16	11 49	0 29	2 2	1 43
21	1 40	18 37	0 44	2 48	2 25	10 1	1 16	11 52	0 27	1 25	1 6
23	1 40	18 37	0 44	2 48	2 25	10 3	1 17	11 55	0 25	0 48	0 S 29
25	1 40	18 38	0 44	2 47	2 24	10 5	1 17	11 58	0 23	0 S 11	0N 8
27	1 40	18 38	0 44	2 46	2 24	10 7	1 18	12 1	0 21	0N 26	0 45
29	1 40	18 39	0 44	2 46	2 23	10 9	1 18	12 3	0 19	1 3	1N 22
31	1N 40	18 S 39	0N 44	2 S 45	2 S 23	10N 12	1N 18	12 S 5	0 S 17	1N 40	

D M	D W	Sidereal Time	☉ Long.	☉ Dec.	☽ Long.	☽ Lat.	☽ Dec.	MIDNIGHT ☽ Long.	MIDNIGHT ☽ Dec.
		H. M. S.	° ′ ″	° ′	° ′ ″	° ′	° ′	° ′ ″	° ′
1	Th	18 42 54	10 ♑ 39 55	23 S 1	17 ♎ 0 50	2 S 46	9 S 15	23 ♎ 26 3	12 S 6
2	F	18 46 50	11 41 5	22 56	29 57 50	3 40	14 53	6 ♏ 36 38	17 33
3	S	18 50 47	12 42 15	22 50	13 ♏ 22 48	4 23	20 2	20 16 34	22 18
4	S	18 54 43	13 43 25	22 44	27 17 56	4 52	24 18	4 ♐ 26 45	25 58
5	M	18 58 40	14 44 36	22 38	11 ♐ 42 37	5 4	27 13	19 4 55	28 2
6	Tu	19 2 36	15 45 46	22 31	26 32 48	4 57	28 21	4 ♑ 5 13	28 8
7	W	19 6 33	16 46 57	22 23	11 ♑ 40 55	4 29	27 24	19 18 36	26 8
8	Th	19 10 30	17 48 8	22 16	26 56 50	3 41	24 23	4 ♒ 34 15	22 13
9	F	19 14 26	18 49 18	22 7	12 ♒ 9 32	2 38	19 41	19 41 28	16 51
10	S	19 18 23	19 50 28	21 59	27 9 3	1 25	13 47	4 ♓ 31 27	10 34
11	S	19 22 19	20 51 37	21 50	11 ♓ 48 2	0 S 7	7 15	18 48 26	3 S 53
12	M	19 26 16	21 52 46	21 40	26 2 23	1N 9	0 S 31	2 ♈ 59 52	2 48
13	Tu	19 30 12	22 53 54	21 30	9 ♈ 50 59	2 19	6 2	16 35 56	9 9
14	W	19 34 9	23 55 1	21 20	23 15 1	3 19	12 7	29 48 36	14 55
15	Th	19 38 5	24 56 7	21 9	6 ♉ 17 7	4 7	17 30	12 ♉ 40 59	19 52
16	F	19 42 2	25 57 13	20 58	19 0 37	4 42	21 59	25 16 29	23 50
17	S	19 45 59	26 58 19	20 46	1 ♊ 28 57	5 2	25 23	7 ♊ 38 25	26 38
18	S	19 49 55	27 59 23	20 34	13 45 15	5 8	27 33	19 49 46	28 8
19	M	19 53 52	29 ♑ 0 27	20 22	25 52 15	5 0	28 23	1 ♋ 53 0	28 17
20	Tu	19 57 48	0 ♒ 1 30	20 9	7 ♋ 52 14	4 39	27 51	13 50 10	27 6
21	W	20 1 45	1 2 32	19 56	19 47 2	4 6	26 2	25 43 1	24 42
22	Th	20 5 41	2 3 33	19 42	1 ♌ 38 20	3 22	23 5	7 ♌ 33 10	21 14
23	F	20 9 38	3 4 34	19 28	13 27 45	2 29	19 10	19 22 18	16 56
24	S	20 13 34	4 5 34	19 14	25 17 6	1 31	14 31	1 12 25	11 58
25	S	20 17 31	5 6 33	19 0	7 ♍ 8 36	0N 27	9 19	13 ♍ 5 59	6 34
26	M	20 21 28	6 7 31	18 45	19 4 57	0 S 38	3N 45	25 5 57	0N 53
27	Tu	20 25 24	7 8 29	18 29	1 ♎ 9 26	1 42	2S 1	7 ♎ 15 53	4 S 55
28	W	20 29 21	8 9 26	18 14	13 25 50	2 43	7 48	19 39 49	10 38
29	Th	20 33 17	9 10 23	17 58	25 58 22	3 37	13 24	2 ♏ 22 0	16 4
30	F	20 37 14	10 11 19	17 42	8 ♏ 51 14	4 22	18 35	15 23 32	20 56
31	S	20 41 10	11 ♒ 12 14	17 S 25	22 ♏ 8 16	4 S 54	23N 3	28 ♏ 56 47	24N 53

First Quarter—January 14*d*, 1*h*. 19*m*. *p.m.*

Full Moon—January 22*d*, 0*h*. 56*m*. *p.m.*

EPHEMERIS] **JANUARY, 1970** 3

D M	Venus Lat.	Venus Dec.	Venus Dec.	Mercury Lat.	Mercury Dec.	Mercury Dec.	☽ Node
	° ′	° ′	° ′	° ′	° ′	° ′	° ′
1	0 S 17	23 S 37		0 S 23	20 S 41		15 ♓ 16
			23 S 37			20 S 21	
3	0 22	23 35		0 N 9	20 1		15 9
			23 33			19 43	
5	0 26	23 30		0 45	19 27		15 3
			23 26			19 12	
7	0 31	23 21		1 23	19 0		14 56
			23 16			18 50	
9	0 35	23 10		2 1	18 42		14 50
			23 3			18 37	
11	0 39	22 56		2 35	18 33		14 44
			22 48			18 32	
13	0 44	22 39		3 2	18 33		14 37
			22 29			18 36	
15	0 48	22 19		3 19	18 40		14 31
			22 8			18 45	
17	0 52	21 57		3 28	18 51		14 25
			21 44			18 59	
19	0 55	21 31		3 25	19 7		14 18
			21 18			19 15	
21	0 59	21 4		3 16	19 24		14 13
			20 49			19 33	
23	1 2	20 34		3 1	19 42		14 6
			20 18			19 52	
25	1 5	20 1		2 43	20 1		13 59
			19 44			20 10	
27	1 9	19 26		2 23	20 18		13 53
			19 8			20 26	
29	1 11	18 49		2 1	20 34		13 47
			18 S 29			20 S 41	
31	1 S 14	18 S 9		1 N 40	20 S 47		13 ♓ 40

Mutual Aspects

2. ♀⊥♆.
3. ☿✱♆. ♄Stat.
4. ☿Stat, ∠ ♂. ♀□♅.
5. ☉Q♃, ∠♆.
7. ♂∠♄. 8. ☉✱♂.
9. ☿△♇. ♀Q♃, ∠♆. [♂Q♃. ♃⊥♇.
11. ☿P♆.
13. ☉☌☿. ♅ Stat.
14. ☿☌♀, ✱♂, P♆.
16. ♀✱♂. ♂P♅.
17. ☉△♇. 18. ☿Q♃.
19. ♀△♇. ♂⊥♄.
20. ☉✱♆. ☿Q♂, ∠♆.
21. ♀✱♆. ♂☍♇.
22. ☉P☿, □♄.
23. ♀□♄. ♂±♃.
24. ☉☌♀. ☿ Stat.
25. ☉□♃. ☿P♀. ♀□♃.
26. ☉P♆. [♂△♆.
28. ♀△♅. ♂⊻♄.
29. ☉△♅.
30. ☿∠♆. ♀P♆, Q♇.
31. ♀Q♆.

D M	♆ Long.	♅ Long.	♄ Long.	♃ Long.	♂ Long.	♀ Long.	☿ Long.	☉	♇	♆	♅	♄	♃	♂	♀	☿
	° ′	° ′	° ′	° ′	° ′	° ′	° ′									
1	29 ♏ 54	8 ♎ 44	2 ♉ 4	2 ♏ 24	12 ♓ 37	5 ♑ 6	29 ♑ 17			∠						
2	29 56	8 44	2 ℞ 3	2 32	13 22	6 21	29 42		⊻	⊻		☍	☌	Q		□
3	29 ♏ 58	8 45	2 3	2 40	14 6	7 37	29 56	✱	∠		⊻			△	✱	
S	0 ♐ 0	8 45	2 D 3	2 48	14 51	8 52	0 ♒ 0	∠	✱	☌	∠		⊻		∠	✱
5	0 2	8 46	2 3	2 55	15 36	10 8	29 ♑ 52	⊻			✱	Q	∠	□	⊻	∠
6	0 3	8 46	2 4	3 3	16 21	11 23	29 ℞ 33		□	⊻		△	✱			⊻
7	0 5	8 47	2 4	3 10	17 5	12 39	29 2	☌		∠	□			✱	☌	
8	0 7	8 47	2 4	3 18	17 50	13 54	28 19		△	✱		□	□	∠		☌
9	0 8	8 47	2 5	3 25	18 35	15 10	27 25	⊻	Q		△			⊻	⊻	
10	0 10	8 47	2 6	3 32	19 19	16 25	26 23			□	Q	✱	△		∠	⊻
S	0 12	8 47	2 6	3 39	20 4	17 41	25 12	∠				∠	Q		✱	∠
12	0 13	8 48	2 8	3 45	20 49	18 56	23 56	✱	☍	△		⊻		☌		✱
13	0 15	8 ℞ 48	2 8	3 52	21 33	20 12	22 37			Q	☍					
14	0 16	8 48	2 10	3 58	22 18	21 27	21 18	□						⊻	□	□
15	0 18	8 47	2 11	4 5	23 3	22 42	20 1		Q			☌	☍	∠		
16	0 19	8 47	2 12	4 11	23 47	23 58	18 48				Q			✱	△	△
17	0 20	8 47	2 14	4 17	24 32	25 13	17 41	△	△	☍		⊻				Q
S	0 22	8 47	2 15	4 22	25 16	26 29	16 41	Q			△	∠	Q		Q	
19	0 23	8 46	2 17	4 28	26 1	27 44	15 50		□					□		
20	0 25	8 46	2 19	4 34	26 45	29 0	15 8				□	✱	△			
21	0 26	8 46	2 21	4 39	27 30	0 ♒ 15	14 36			Q						☍
22	0 27	8 45	2 23	4 44	28 14	1 30	14 12	☍	✱	△		□	□	△	☍	
23	0 29	8 44	2 25	4 49	28 58	2 46	13 58		∠		✱			Q		
24	0 30	8 44	2 27	4 54	29 43	4 1	13 D 52		⊻	□	∠					Q
S	0 31	8 43	2 30	4 58	0 ♈ 27	5 17	13 55				⊻	△	✱			
26	0 32	8 42	2 32	5 3	1 12	6 32	14 5	Q				Q	∠		Q	△
27	0 33	8 42	2 34	5 7	1 56	7 47	14 22		☌	✱			⊻	☍		
28	0 34	8 41	2 37	5 12	2 40	9 3	14 45	△		∠	☌				△	□
29	0 36	8 40	2 40	5 16	3 24	10 18	15 14		⊻	⊻						
30	0 37	8 39	2 43	5 19	4 9	11 33	15 49	□	∠		⊻	☍	☌		□	
31	0 ♐ 38	8 ♎ 38	2 ♉ 46	5 ♏ 23	4 ♈ 53	12 ♒ 49	16 ♑ 29		✱		∠			Q		✱

Last Quarter—January 30*d*, 2*h*. 39*m*. *p.m.*

NEW MOON—February 23, 9*h*. 13*m*. *p.m*. (4° ♓ 56′)

D M	D W	Sidereal Time	☉ Long.	☉ Dec.	☽ Long.	☽ Lat.	☽ Dec.	☽ Node	MIDNIGHT ☽ Long.	MIDNIGHT ☽ Dec.
		H. M. S.	° ′ ″	° ′	° ′ ″	° ′	° ′	° ′	° ′ ″	° ′
1	M	20 45 28	12♒18 16	17S 7	10♉57 52	4S 59	10N22	21♋31	17♉59 0	12N38
2	Tu	20 49 24	13 19 9	16 49	25 3 12	4 26	14 44	21 28	2♊10 17	16 38
3	W	20 53 21	14 20 0	16 32	9♊20 0	3 36	18 18	21 25	16 32 1	19 42
4	Th	20 57 17	15 20 50	16 14	23 45 57	2 31	20 47	21 22	1♋1 21	21 31
5	F	21 1 14	16 21 39	15 56	8♋17 38	1S 17	21 54	21 18	15 34 14	21 55
6	S	21 5 11	17 22 26	15 38	22 50 26	0N 3	21 33	21 15	0♌5 33	20 49
7	Su	21 9 7	18 23 12	15 19	7♌18 50	1 21	19 45	21 12	14 29 34	18 22
8	M	21 13 4	19 23 57	15 0	21 37 2	2 34	16 43	21 9	28 40 37	14 51
9	Tu	21 17 0	20 24 40	14 41	5♍39 42	3 36	12 46	21 6	12♍33 51	10 33
10	W	21 20 57	21 25 22	14 22	19 22 40	4 23	8 14	21 3	26 5 54	5 51
11	Th	21 24 53	22 26 3	14 2	2♎43 26	4 55	3N26	20 59	9♎15 17	1N 0
12	F	21 28 50	23 26 42	13 42	15 41 31	5 11	1S 24	20 56	22 2 24	3S 45
13	S	21 32 46	24 27 21	13 22	28 18 13	5 11	6 2	20 53	4♏29 24	8 13
14	Su	21 36 43	25 27 58	13 2	10♏36 24	4 56	10 19	20 50	16 39 46	12 17
15	M	21 40 40	26 28 34	12 41	22 40 5	4 29	14 6	20 47	28 37 56	15 47
16	Tu	21 44 36	27 29 9	12 21	4♐33 59	3 50	17 17	20 44	10♐28 51	18 36
17	W	21 48 33	28 29 43	12 0	16 23 12	3 2	19 44	20 40	22 17 39	20 38
18	Th	21 52 29	29♒30 15	11 39	28 12 51	2 6	21 20	20 37	4♑9 23	21 47
19	F	21 56 26	0♓30 47	11 18	10♑7 50	1N 4	21 59	20 34	16 8 42	21 56
20	S	22 0 22	1 31 17	10 56	22 12 28	0S 1	21 38	20 31	28 19 33	21 4
21	Su	22 4 19	2 31 45	10 34	4♒30 19	1 8	20 14	20 28	10♒45 3	19 9
22	M	22 8 15	3 32 12	10 13	17 3 58	2 12	17 49	20 24	23 27 10	16 15
23	Tu	22 12 12	4 32 37	9 51	29 54 44	3 11	14 29	20 21	6♓26 37	12 30
24	W	22 16 9	5 33 1	9 29	13♓2 42	4 1	10 22	20 18	19 42 48	8 5
25	Th	22 20 5	6 33 23	9 6	26 26 40	4 39	5 41	20 15	3♈13 59	3S 11
26	F	22 24 1	7 33 43	8 44	10♈4 26	5 2	0S 38	20 12	16 57 39	1N56
27	S	22 27 58	8 34 1	8 22	23 53 14	5 8	4N30	20 9	0♉50 51	7 2
28	Su	22 31 55	9♓34 18	7S 59	7♉50 7	4S 55	9N28	20♋5	14♉50 46	11N48

D M	Mercury Lat.	Mercury Dec.	Mercury Dec.	Venus Lat.	Venus Dec.	Venus Dec.	Mars Lat.	Mars Dec.	Mars Dec.	Jupiter Lat.	Jupiter Dec.
	° ′	° ′	° ′	° ′	° ′	° ′	° ′	° ′	° ′	° ′	° ′
1	3N32	13S 55	14S 11	7N32	13S 42	13S 44	2N50	4S 6	4S 10	1N16	13S 28
3	3 38	14 28	14 46	7 33	13 47	13 50	2 51	4 13	4 17	1 16	13 30
5	3 36	15 4	15 22	7 32	13 53	13 57	2 53	4 20	4 22	1 17	13 32
7	3 25	15 41	15 58	7 28	14 1	14 5	2 55	4 25	4 28	1 17	13 34
9	3 8	16 15	16 31	7 22	14 9	14 13	2 57	4 30	4 32	1 18	13 35
11	2 47	16 45	16 59	7 14	14 17	14 21	2 59	4 33	4 35	1 18	13 36
13	2 24	17 11	17 22	7 5	14 25	14 29	3 1	4 36	4 37	1 19	13 37
15	1 59	17 31	17 39	6 54	14 33	14 37	3 2	4 38	4 38	1 19	13 38
17	1 34	17 46	17 51	6 41	14 41	14 45	3 4	4 39	4 39	1 19	13 38
19	1 10	17 54	17 57	6 28	14 48	14 51	3 6	4 38	4 38	1 20	13 39
21	0 46	17 58	17 57	6 14	14 54	14 57	3 7	4 37	4 36	1 20	13 39
23	0 24	17 55	17S 52	6 0	15 0	15S 2	3 9	4 35	4S 33	1 21	13 39
25	0N 2	17 47		5 45	15 4		3 10	4 32		1 21	13 38
26	0S 8	17 41		5 37	15 6		3 10	4 30		1 21	13 38
27	0 18	17 33		5 30	15 7		3 11	4 27		1 21	13 38
28	0S 27	17S 24		5N22	15S 8		3N12	4S 25		1N22	13S 37

FIRST QUARTER—February 1, 2*h*. 28*m*. *p.m*. (12° ♉ 25′)

Full Moon—February 8, 7*h.* 57*m.* *a.m.* (19° ♌ 14′)

EPHEMERIS]				FEBRUARY, 1982				5									
D	☿	♀	♂	♃	♄	♅	♆	♇	Lunar Aspects								
M	Long.	Long.	Long.	Long.	Long.	Long.	Long.	Long.	☉	☿	♀	♂	♃	♄	♅	♆	♇
	° ′	° ′	° ′	° ′	° ′	° ′	° ′	° ′									
1	11♒32	25♑10	17♎ 5	9♏32	22♎15	4♐ 2	26♐12	26♎56	□	□			☍			Q	
2	10 ℞18	24 ℞48	17 17	9 36	22 ℞15	4 4	26 14	26 ℞56			△						
3	9 6	24 29	17 29	9 40	22 14	4 6	26 15	26 56	△	△	Q	Q		Q	☍		Q
4	7 57	24 12	17 40	9 43	22 14	4 8	26 17	26 55	Q	Q		△	Q	△		☍	△
5	6 54	23 57	17 50	9 47	22 13	4 9	26 19	26 55					△				
6	5 56	23 45	18 0	9 50	22 13	4 11	26 20	26 55			☍	□		□	Q		□
7	5 6	23 36	18 9	9 53	22 12	4 13	26 22	26 55		☍			□		△	Q	
8	4 24	23 29	18 18	9 56	22 11	4 14	26 23	26 54	☍			*		*		△	*
9	3 50	23 24	18 26	9 59	22 10	4 16	26 25	26 54			Q	∠	*	∠	□		∠
10	3 25	23 22	18 33	10 2	22 9	4 17	26 26	26 53		Q	△	⊻	∠	⊻			
11	3 7	23 D22	18 40	10 4	22 8	4 19	26 28	26 53	Q	△					*	□	⊻
12	2 58	23 25	18 46	10 7	22 7	4 20	26 29	26 53				☌	⊻		∠		
13	2 D55	23 30	18 52	10 9	22 5	4 22	26 31	26 52	△	□	□			☌	⊻	*	☌
14	3 0	23 38	18 56	10 11	22 4	4 23	26 32	26 51					☌			∠	
15	3 12	23 47	19 1	10 13	22 2	4 24	26 33	26 51	□		*	⊻		⊻		⊻	⊻
16	3 29	23 59	19 4	10 14	22 1	4 25	26 35	26 50		*	∠	∠	⊻	∠	☌		
17	3 53	24 13	19 7	10 15	21 59	4 26	26 36	26 50		∠		*		*			∠
18	4 22	24 29	19 9	10 17	21 57	4 27	26 37	26 49	*		⊻		∠			☌	*
19	4 56	24 47	19 10	10 18	21 55	4 28	26 39	26 48	∠	⊻			*		⊻		
20	5 34	25 8	19 11	10 18	21 53	4 29	26 40	26 48			☌	□		□	∠	⊻	□
21	6 16	25 30	19 ℞11	10 19	21 51	4 30	26 41	26 47	⊻	☌			□		*		
22	7 3	25 53	19 10	10 19	21 49	4 31	26 42	26 46				△		△		∠	
23	7 53	26 19	19 8	10 20	21 47	4 32	26 43	26 45	☌		⊻	Q			□	*	△
24	8 46	26 46	19 6	10 ℞20	21 44	4 33	26 44	26 44		⊻	∠		△	Q			Q
25	9 42	27 15	19 2	10 20	21 42	4 33	26 46	26 43		∠	*		Q			□	
26	10 41	27 45	18 58	10 19	21 39	4 34	26 47	26 42	⊻	*					△		
27	11 43	28 17	18 54	10 19	21 36	4 35	26 48	26 41	∠		□	☍		☍	Q	△	☍
28	12♒47	28♑50	18♎48	10♏18	21♎34	4♐35	26♐49	26♎40	*	□			☍			Q	

D	Saturn		Uranus		Neptune		Pluto	
M	Lat.	Dec.	Lat.	Dec.	Lat.	Dec.	Lat.	Dec.
	° ′	° ′	° ′	° ′	° ′	° ′	° ′	° ′
1	2 N34	6 S 17	0 N10	20 S 48	1 N16	22 S 7	17 N14	5 N43
3	2 35	6 16	0 10	20 48	1 16	22 8	17 15	5 44
5	2 35	6 15	0 10	20 49	1 16	22 8	17 16	5 46
7	2 36	6 14	0 10	20 49	1 16	22 8	17 17	5 47
9	2 36	6 13	0 10	20 50	1 16	22 8	17 18	5 48
11	2 37	6 12	0 10	20 51	1 16	22 8	17 19	5 49
13	2 37	6 10	0 10	20 51	1 16	22 8	17 20	5 51
15	2 38	6 8	0 10	20 52	1 16	22 8	17 21	5 52
17	2 38	6 7	0 10	20 52	1 16	22 8	17 22	5 53
19	2 39	6 5	0 10	20 52	1 16	22 8	17 23	5 55
21	2 39	6 3	0 10	20 53	1 16	22 8	17 24	5 56
23	2 40	6 1	0 10	20 53	1 16	22 8	17 25	5 58
25	2 40	5 59	0 10	20 53	1 16	22 8	17 26	5 59
26	2 41	5 57	0 10	20 53	1 16	22 8	17 27	6 0
27	2 41	5 56	0 10	20 54	1 16	22 8	17 27	6 1
28	2 N41	5 S 55	0 N10	20 S 54	1 N17	22 S 8	17 N28	6 N 1

Mutual Aspects

1. ☉ ☌ ☿. ☿ ∠ ♆.
3. ☿ □ ♃.
5. ☉ Q ♅.
6. ☉ P ☿.
7. ☉ △ ♂.
8. ☿ * ♅.
10. ☉ P ♀. ♀ Stat.
11. ☉ △ ♄.
12. ☉ ⊻ ♀, P ♃.
13. ☿ Stat.
15. ☉ * ♆, △ ♇.
18. ☿ * ♅.
19. ☉ ⊥ ♀.
20. ♂ Stat.
23. ☉ Q ♂, □ ♅.
24. ♀ ⊻ ♆, □ ♇. ♃ Stat. ♆ * ♇.
25. ☉ Q ♄. ♄ P ♇.
26. ☿ □ ♃.
27. ☉ Q ♆. ☿ ∠ ♆.

Last Quarter—February 15, 8*h.* 21*m.* *p.m.* (26° ♏ 50′)

TABLES OF HOUSES FOR LONDON, *Latitude* 51° 32′ N.

Sidereal Time H.	M.	S.	10 ♈ °	11 ♉ °	12 ♊ °	Ascen ♋ °	′	2 ♌ °	3 ♍ °
0	0	0	0	9	22	26	36	12	3
0	3	40	1	10	23	27	17	13	3
0	7	20	2	11	24	27	56	14	4
0	11	0	3	12	25	28	42	15	5
0	14	41	4	13	25	29	17	15	6
0	18	21	5	14	26	29	55	16	7
0	22	2	6	15	27	0 ♌	34	17	8
0	25	42	7	16	28	1	14	18	8
0	29	23	8	17	29	1	55	18	9
0	33	4	9	18	♋	2	33	19	10
0	36	45	10	19	1	3	14	20	11
0	40	26	11	20	1	3	54	20	12
0	44	8	12	21	2	4	33	21	13
0	47	50	13	22	3	5	12	22	14
0	51	32	14	23	4	5	52	23	15
0	55	14	15	24	5	6	30	23	15
0	58	57	16	25	6	7	9	24	16
1	2	40	17	26	6	7	50	25	17
1	6	23	18	27	7	8	30	26	18
1	10	7	19	28	8	9	9	26	19
1	13	51	20	29	9	9	48	27	19
1	17	35	21	♊	10	10	28	28	20
1	21	20	22	1	10	11	8	28	21
1	25	6	23	2	11	11	48	29	22
1	28	52	24	3	12	12	28	♍	23
1	32	38	25	4	13	13	8	1	24
1	36	25	26	5	14	13	48	1	25
1	40	12	27	6	14	14	28	2	25
1	44	0	28	7	15	15	8	3	26
1	47	48	29	8	16	15	48	4	27
1	51	37	30	9	17	16	28	4	28

Sidereal Time H.	M.	S.	10 ♉ °	11 ♊ °	12 ♋ °	Ascen ♌ °	′	2 ♍ °	3 ♍ °
1	51	37	0	9	17	16	28	4	28
1	55	27	1	10	18	17	8	5	29
1	59	17	2	11	19	17	48	6	♎
2	3	8	3	12	19	18	28	7	1
2	6	59	4	13	20	19	9	8	2
2	10	51	5	14	21	19	49	9	2
2	14	44	6	15	22	20	29	9	3
2	18	37	7	16	22	21	10	10	4
2	22	31	8	17	23	21	51	11	5
2	26	25	9	18	24	22	32	11	6
2	30	20	10	19	25	23	14	12	7
2	34	16	11	20	25	23	55	13	8
2	38	13	12	21	26	24	36	14	9
2	42	10	13	22	27	25	17	15	10
2	46	8	14	23	28	25	58	15	11
2	50	7	15	24	29	26	40	16	12
2	54	7	16	25	29	27	22	17	12
2	58	7	17	26	♌	28	4	18	13
3	2	8	18	27	1	28	46	18	14
3	6	9	19	27	2	29	28	19	15
3	10	12	20	28	3	0 ♍	12	20	16
3	14	15	21	29	3	0	54	21	17
3	18	19	22	♋	4	1	36	22	18
3	22	23	23	1	5	2	20	22	19
3	26	29	24	2	6	3	2	23	20
3	30	35	25	3	7	3	45	24	21
3	34	41	26	4	7	4	28	25	22
3	38	49	27	5	8	5	11	26	23
3	42	57	28	6	9	5	54	27	24
3	47	6	29	7	10	6	38	27	25
3	51	15	30	8	11	7	21	28	25

Sidereal Time H.	M.	S.	10 ♊ °	11 ♋ °	12 ♌ °	Ascen ♍ °	′	2 ♍ °	3 ♎ °
3	51	15	0	8	11	7	21	28	25
3	55	25	1	9	12	8	5	29	26
3	59	36	2	10	12	8	49	♎	27
4	3	48	3	10	13	9	33	1	28
4	8	0	4	11	14	10	17	2	29
4	12	13	5	12	15	11	2	2	♏
4	16	26	6	13	16	11	46	3	1
4	20	40	7	14	17	12	30	4	2
4	24	55	8	15	17	13	15	5	3
4	29	10	9	16	18	14	0	6	4
4	33	26	10	17	19	14	45	7	5
4	37	42	11	18	20	15	30	8	6
4	41	59	12	19	21	16	15	8	7
4	46	16	13	20	21	17	0	9	8
4	50	34	14	21	22	17	45	10	9
4	54	52	15	22	23	18	30	11	10
4	59	10	16	23	24	19	16	12	11
5	3	29	17	24	25	20	3	13	12
5	7	49	18	25	26	20	49	14	13
5	12	9	19	25	27	21	35	14	14
5	16	29	20	26	28	22	20	15	14
5	20	49	21	27	28	23	6	16	15
5	25	9	22	28	29	23	51	17	16
5	29	30	23	29	♍	24	37	18	17
5	33	51	24	♌	1	25	23	19	18
5	38	12	25	1	2	26	9	20	19
5	42	34	26	2	3	26	55	21	20
5	46	55	27	3	4	27	41	21	21
5	51	17	28	4	4	28	27	22	22
5	55	38	29	5	5	29	13	23	23
6	0	0	30	6	6	30	0	24	24

Sidereal Time H.	M.	S.	10 ♋ °	11 ♌ °	12 ♍ °	Ascen ♎ °	′	2 ♎ °	3 ♏ °
6	0	0	0	6	6	0	0	24	24
6	4	22	1	7	7	0	47	25	25
6	8	43	2	8	8	1	33	26	26
6	13	5	3	9	9	2	19	27	27
6	17	26	4	10	10	3	5	27	28
6	21	48	5	11	10	3	51	28	29
6	26	9	6	12	11	4	37	29	♐
6	30	30	7	13	12	5	23	♏	1
6	34	51	8	14	13	6	9	1	2
6	39	11	9	15	14	6	55	2	3
6	43	31	10	16	15	7	40	2	4
6	47	51	11	16	16	8	26	3	4
6	52	11	12	17	16	9	12	4	5
6	56	31	13	18	17	9	58	5	6
7	0	50	14	19	18	10	43	6	7
7	5	8	15	20	19	11	28	7	8
7	9	26	16	21	20	12	14	8	9
7	13	44	17	22	21	12	59	8	10
7	18	1	18	23	22	13	45	9	11
7	22	18	19	24	23	14	30	10	12
7	26	34	20	25	24	15	15	11	13
7	30	50	21	26	25	16	0	12	14
7	35	5	22	27	25	16	45	13	15
7	39	20	23	28	26	17	30	13	16
7	43	34	24	29	27	18	15	14	17
7	47	47	25	♍	28	18	59	15	18
7	52	0	26	1	29	19	43	16	19
7	56	12	27	2	29	20	27	17	20
8	0	24	28	3	♎	21	11	18	20
8	4	35	29	4	1	21	56	18	21
8	8	45	30	5	2	22	40	19	22

Sidereal Time H.	M.	S.	10 ♌ °	11 ♍ °	12 ♎ °	Ascen ♎ °	′	2 ♏ °	3 ♐ °
8	8	45	0	5	2	22	40	19	22
8	12	54	1	5	3	23	24	20	23
8	17	3	2	6	3	24	7	21	24
8	21	11	3	7	4	24	50	22	25
8	25	19	4	8	5	25	34	23	26
8	29	26	5	9	6	26	18	23	27
8	33	31	6	10	7	27	1	24	28
8	37	37	7	11	8	27	44	25	29
8	41	41	8	12	8	28	26	26	♑
8	45	45	9	13	9	29	8	27	1
8	49	48	10	14	10	29	50	27	2
8	53	51	11	15	11	0 ♏	32	28	3
8	57	52	12	16	12	1	15	29	4
9	1	53	13	17	12	1	58	♐	4
9	5	53	14	18	13	2	39	1	5
9	9	53	15	18	14	3	21	1	6
9	13	52	16	19	15	4	3	2	7
9	17	50	17	20	16	4	44	3	8
9	21	47	18	21	16	5	26	3	9
9	25	44	19	22	17	6	7	4	10
9	29	40	20	23	18	6	48	5	11
9	33	35	21	24	18	7	29	5	12
9	37	29	22	25	19	8	9	6	13
9	41	23	23	26	20	8	50	7	14
9	45	16	24	27	21	9	31	8	15
9	49	9	25	28	22	10	11	9	16
9	53	1	26	28	23	10	51	9	17
9	56	52	27	29	23	11	32	10	18
10	0	43	28	♎	24	12	12	11	19
10	4	3[illegible]	29	1	25	12	53	12	20
10	8	2[illegible]	30	2	26	13	33	13	20

Sidereal Time H.	M.	S.	10 ♍ °	11 ♎ °	12 ♎ °	Ascen ♏ °	′	2 ♐ °	3 ♑ °
10	8	23	0	2	26	13	33	13	20
10	12	12	1	3	26	14	13	14	21
10	16	0	2	4	27	14	53	15	22
10	19	48	3	5	28	15	33	15	23
10	23	35	4	5	29	16	13	16	24
10	27	22	5	6	29	16	52	17	25
10	31	8	6	7	♏	17	32	18	26
10	34	54	7	8	1	18	12	19	27
10	38	40	8	9	2	18	52	20	28
10	42	25	9	10	2	19	31	20	29
10	46	9	10	11	3	20	11	21	♒
10	49	53	11	11	4	20	50	22	1
10	53	37	12	12	4	21	30	23	2
10	57	20	13	13	5	22	9	24	3
11	1	3	14	14	6	22	49	24	4
11	4	46	15	15	7	23	28	25	5
11	8	28	16	16	7	24	8	26	6
11	12	10	17	17	8	24	47	27	8
11	15	52	18	17	9	25	27	28	9
11	19	34	19	18	10	26	6	29	10
11	23	15	20	19	10	26	45	♑	11
11	26	56	21	20	11	27	25	0	12
11	30	37	22	21	12	28	5	1	13
11	34	18	23	22	13	28	44	2	14
11	37	58	24	23	13	29	24	3	15
11	41	39	25	23	14	0 ♐	3	4	16
11	45	19	26	24	15	0	43	5	17
11	49	0	27	25	15	1	23	6	18
11	52	40	28	26	16	2	3	6	19
11	56	20	29	27	17	2	43	7	20
12	0	0	30	27	17	3	23	8	21

TABLES OF HOUSES FOR LONDON, Latitude 51° 32′ *N.*

Sidereal Time H.	M.	S.	10 ♎ °	11 ♎ °	12 ♏ °	Ascen ♐ °	′	2 ♑ °	3 ♒ °
12	0	0	0	27	17	3	23	8	21
12	3	40	1	28	18	4	4	9	23
12	7	20	2	29	19	4	45	10	24
12	11	0	3	♏	20	5	26	11	25
12	14	41	4	1	20	6	7	12	26
12	18	21	5	1	21	6	48	13	27
12	22	2	6	2	22	7	29	14	28
12	25	42	7	3	23	8	10	15	29
12	29	23	8	4	23	8	51	16	♓
12	33	4	9	5	24	9	33	17	2
12	36	45	10	6	25	10	15	18	3
12	40	26	11	6	25	10	57	19	4
12	44	8	12	7	26	11	40	20	5
12	47	50	13	8	27	12	22	21	6
12	51	32	14	9	28	13	4	22	7
12	55	14	15	10	28	13	47	23	9
12	58	57	16	11	29	14	30	24	10
13	2	40	17	11	♐	15	14	25	11
13	6	23	18	12	1	15	59	26	12
13	10	7	19	13	1	16	44	27	13
13	13	51	20	14	2	17	29	28	15
13	17	35	21	15	3	18	14	29	16
13	21	20	22	16	4	19	0	♒	17
13	25	6	23	16	4	19	45	1	18
13	28	52	24	17	5	20	31	2	20
13	32	38	25	18	6	21	18	4	21
13	36	25	26	19	7	22	6	5	22
13	40	12	27	20	7	22	54	6	23
13	44	0	28	21	8	23	42	7	25
13	47	48	29	21	9	24	31	8	26
13	51	37	30	22	10	25	20	10	27

Sidereal Time H.	M.	S.	10 ♏ °	11 ♏ °	12 ♐ °	Ascen ♐ °	′	2 ♒ °	3 ♓ °
13	51	37	0	22	10	25	20	10	27
13	55	27	1	23	11	26	10	11	28
13	59	17	2	24	11	27	2	12	♈
14	3	8	3	25	12	27	53	14	1
14	6	59	4	26	13	28	45	15	2
14	10	51	5	26	14	29	36	16	4
14	14	44	6	27	15	0 ♑	29	18	5
14	18	37	7	28	15	1	23	19	6
14	22	31	8	29	16	2	18	20	8
14	26	25	9	♐	17	3	14	22	9
14	30	20	10	1	18	4	11	23	10
14	34	16	11	2	19	5	9	25	11
14	38	13	12	2	20	6	7	26	13
14	42	10	13	3	20	7	6	28	14
14	46	8	14	4	21	8	6	29	15
14	50	7	15	5	22	9	8	♓	17
14	54	7	16	6	23	10	11	2	18
14	58	7	17	7	24	11	15	4	19
15	2	8	18	8	25	12	20	6	21
15	6	9	19	9	26	13	27	8	22
15	10	12	20	9	27	14	35	9	23
15	14	15	21	10	27	15	43	11	24
15	18	19	22	11	28	16	52	13	26
15	22	23	23	12	29	18	3	14	27
15	26	29	24	13	♑	19	16	16	28
15	30	35	25	14	1	20	32	17	29
15	34	41	26	15	2	21	48	19	♉
15	38	49	27	16	3	23	8	21	2
15	42	57	28	17	4	24	29	22	3
15	47	6	29	18	5	25	51	24	5
15	51	15	30	18	6	27	15	26	6

Sidereal Time H.	M.	S.	10 ♐ °	11 ♐ °	12 ♑ °	Ascen ♑ °	′	2 ♓ °	3 ♉ °
15	51	15	0	18	6	27	15	26	6
15	55	25	1	19	7	28	42	28	7
15	59	36	2	20	8	0 ♒	11	♈	9
16	3	48	3	21	9	1	42	2	10
16	8	0	4	22	10	3	16	3	11
16	12	13	5	23	11	4	53	5	12
16	16	26	6	24	12	6	32	7	14
16	20	40	7	25	13	8	13	9	15
16	24	55	8	26	14	9	57	11	16
16	29	10	9	27	16	11	44	12	17
16	33	26	10	28	17	13	34	14	18
16	37	42	11	29	18	15	26	16	20
16	41	59	12	♑	19	17	20	18	21
16	46	16	13	1	20	19	18	20	22
16	50	34	14	2	21	21	22	21	23
16	54	52	15	3	22	23	29	23	25
16	59	10	16	4	24	25	36	25	26
17	3	29	17	5	25	27	46	27	27
17	7	49	18	6	26	0 ♓	0	28	28
17	12	9	19	7	27	2	19	♉	29
17	16	29	20	8	29	4	40	2	♊
17	20	49	21	9	♒	7	2	3	1
17	25	9	22	10	1	9	26	5	2
17	29	30	23	11	3	11	54	7	3
17	33	51	24	12	4	14	24	8	5
17	38	12	25	13	5	17	0	10	6
17	42	34	26	14	7	19	33	11	7
17	46	55	27	15	8	22	6	13	8
17	51	17	28	16	10	24	40	14	9
17	55	38	29	17	11	27	20	16	10
18	0	0	30	18	13	30	0	17	11

Sidereal Time H.	M.	S.	10 ♑ °	11 ♑ °	12 ♒ °	Ascen ♈ °	′	2 ♉ °	3 ♊ °
18	0	0	0	18	13	0	0	17	11
18	4	22	1	20	14	2	39	19	13
18	8	43	2	21	16	5	19	20	14
18	13	5	3	22	17	7	55	22	15
18	17	26	4	23	19	10	29	23	16
18	21	48	5	24	20	13	2	25	17
18	26	9	6	25	22	15	36	26	18
18	30	30	7	26	23	18	6	28	19
18	34	51	8	27	25	20	34	29	20
18	39	11	9	29	27	22	59	♊	21
18	43	31	10	♒	28	25	22	1	22
18	47	51	11	1	♓	27	42	2	23
18	52	11	12	2	2	29	58	4	24
18	56	31	13	3	3	2 ♉	13	5	25
19	0	50	14	4	5	4	24	6	26
19	5	8	15	6	7	6	30	8	27
19	9	26	16	7	9	8	36	9	28
19	13	44	17	8	10	10	40	10	29
19	18	1	18	9	12	12	39	11	♋
19	22	18	19	10	14	14	35	12	1
19	26	34	20	12	16	16	28	13	2
19	30	50	21	13	18	18	17	14	3
19	35	5	22	14	19	20	3	16	4
19	39	20	23	15	21	21	48	17	5
19	43	34	24	16	23	23	29	18	6
19	47	47	25	18	25	25	9	19	7
19	52	0	26	19	27	26	45	20	8
19	56	12	27	20	28	28	18	21	9
20	0	24	28	21	♈	29	49	22	10
20	4	35	29	23	2	1 ♊	19	23	11
20	8	45	30	24	4	2	45	24	12

Sidereal Time H.	M.	S.	10 ♒ °	11 ♒ °	12 ♈ °	Ascen ♊ °	′	2 ♊ °	3 ♋ °
20	8	45	0	24	4	2	45	24	12
20	12	54	1	25	6	4	9	25	12
20	17	3	2	27	7	5	32	26	13
20	21	11	3	28	9	6	53	27	14
20	25	19	4	29	11	8	12	28	15
20	29	26	5	♓	13	9	27	29	16
20	33	31	6	2	14	10	43	♋	17
20	37	37	7	3	16	11	58	1	18
20	41	41	8	4	18	13	9	2	19
20	45	45	9	6	19	14	18	3	20
20	49	48	10	7	21	15	25	3	21
20	53	51	11	8	23	16	32	4	21
20	57	52	12	9	24	17	39	5	22
21	1	53	13	11	26	18	44	6	23
21	5	53	14	12	28	19	48	7	24
21	9	53	15	13	29	20	51	8	25
21	13	52	16	15	♉	21	53	9	26
21	17	50	17	16	2	22	53	10	27
21	21	47	18	17	4	23	52	10	28
21	25	44	19	19	5	24	51	11	28
21	29	40	20	20	7	25	48	12	29
21	33	35	21	22	8	26	44	13	♌
21	37	29	22	23	10	27	40	14	1
21	41	23	23	24	11	28	34	15	2
21	45	16	24	25	13	29	29	15	3
21	49	9	25	26	14	0 ♋	22	16	4
21	53	1	26	28	15	1	15	17	4
21	56	52	27	29	16	2	7	18	5
22	0	43	28	♈	18	2	57	19	6
22	4	33	29	2	19	3	48	19	7
22	8	23	30	3	20	4	38	20	8

Sidereal Time H.	M.	S.	10 ♓ °	11 ♈ °	12 ♉ °	Ascen ♋ °	′	2 ♋ °	3 ♌ °
22	8	23	0	3	20	4	38	20	8
22	12	12	1	4	21	5	28	21	8
22	16	0	2	6	23	6	17	22	9
22	19	48	3	7	24	7	5	23	10
22	23	35	4	8	25	7	53	23	11
22	27	22	5	9	26	8	42	24	12
22	31	8	6	10	28	9	29	25	13
22	34	54	7	12	29	10	16	26	14
22	38	40	8	13	♊	11	2	26	14
22	42	25	9	14	1	11	47	27	15
22	46	9	10	15	2	12	31	28	16
22	49	53	11	17	3	13	16	29	17
22	53	37	12	18	4	14	1	29	18
22	57	20	13	19	5	14	45	♌	19
23	1	3	14	20	6	15	28	1	19
23	4	46	15	21	7	16	11	2	20
23	8	28	16	23	8	16	54	2	21
23	12	10	17	24	9	17	37	3	22
23	15	52	18	25	10	18	20	4	23
23	19	34	19	26	11	19	3	5	24
23	23	15	20	27	12	19	45	5	24
23	26	56	21	29	13	20	26	6	25
23	30	37	22	♉	14	21	8	7	26
23	34	18	23	1	15	21	50	7	27
23	37	58	24	2	16	22	31	8	28
23	41	39	25	3	17	23	12	9	28
23	45	19	26	4	18	23	53	9	29
23	49	0	27	5	19	24	32	10	♍
23	52	40	28	6	20	25	15	11	1
23	56	20	29	8	21	25	56	12	2
24	0	0	30	9	22	26	36	13	3

TABLES OF HOUSES FOR LIVERPOOL, Latitude 53° 25′ N

Sidereal Time.			10 ♎	11 ♎	12 ♏	Ascen ♐		2 ♑	3 ♒
H.	M.	S.	°	°	°	°	′	°	°
12	0	0	0	27	16	1	48	6	21
12	3	40	1	28	17	2	27	7	22
12	7	20	2	29	18	3	6	8	23
12	11	0	3	♏	18	3	46	9	24
12	14	41	4	0	19	4	25	10	25
12	18	21	5	1	20	5	6	10	26
12	22	2	6	2	21	5	46	11	28
12	25	42	7	3	21	6	26	12	29
12	29	23	8	4	22	7	6	13	♓
12	33	4	9	4	23	7	46	14	1
12	36	45	10	5	24	8	27	15	2
12	40	26	11	6	24	9	8	16	3
12	44	8	12	7	25	9	49	17	5
12	47	50	13	8	26	10	30	18	6
12	51	32	14	9	26	11	12	19	7
12	55	14	15	9	27	11	54	20	8
12	58	57	16	10	28	12	36	21	10
13	2	40	17	11	28	13	19	22	11
13	6	23	18	12	29	14	2	23	12
13	10	7	19	13	♐	14	45	25	13
13	13	51	20	13	1	15	28	26	15
13	17	35	21	14	1	16	12	27	16
13	21	20	22	15	2	16	56	28	17
13	25	6	23	16	3	17	41	29	18
13	28	52	24	17	4	18	26	♒	19
13	32	38	25	17	4	19	11	1	21
13	36	25	26	18	5	19	57	3	22
13	40	12	27	19	6	20	44	4	23
13	44	0	28	20	7	21	31	5	24
13	47	48	29	21	7	22	18	7	26
13	51	37	30	21	8	23	6	8	27

Sidereal Time.			10 ♏	11 ♏	12 ♐	Ascen ♐		2 ♒	3 ♓
H.	M.	S.	°	°	°	°	′	°	°
13	51	37	0	21	8	23	6	8	27
13	55	27	1	22	9	23	55	9	28
13	59	17	2	23	10	24	43	10	♈
14	3	8	3	24	10	25	33	12	1
14	6	59	4	25	11	26	23	13	2
14	10	51	5	26	12	27	14	15	4
14	14	44	6	26	13	28	6	16	5
14	18	37	7	27	13	28	59	18	6
14	22	31	8	28	14	29	52	19	8
14	26	25	9	29	15	0 ♑	46	20	9
14	30	20	10	♐	16	1	41	22	10
14	34	16	11	1	17	2	36	23	11
14	38	13	12	2	18	3	33	25	13
14	42	10	13	2	18	4	30	26	14
14	46	8	14	3	19	5	29	28	16
14	50	7	15	4	20	6	29	♓	17
14	54	7	16	5	21	7	30	1	18
14	58	7	17	6	22	8	32	3	20
15	2	8	18	7	23	9	35	5	21
15	6	9	19	8	24	10	39	6	22
15	10	12	20	8	24	11	45	8	23
15	14	15	21	9	25	12	52	10	25
15	18	19	22	10	26	14	1	11	26
15	22	23	23	11	27	15	11	13	27
15	26	29	24	12	28	16	23	15	29
15	30	35	25	13	29	17	37	17	♉
15	34	41	26	14	♑	18	53	19	1
15	38	49	27	15	1	20	10	21	3
15	42	57	28	16	2	21	29	22	4
15	47	6	29	16	3	22	51	24	5
15	51	15	30	17	4	24	15	26	7

Sidereal Time.			10 ♐	11 ♐	12 ♑	Ascen ♑		2 ♓	3 ♉
H.	M.	S.	°	°	°	°	′	°	°
15	51	15	0	17	4	24	15	26	7
15	55	25	1	18	5	25	41	28	8
15	59	36	2	19	6	27	10	♈	9
16	3	48	3	20	7	28	41	2	10
16	8	0	4	21	8	0 ♒	14	4	12
16	12	13	5	22	9	1	50	5	13
16	16	26	6	23	10	3	30	7	14
16	20	40	7	24	11	5	13	9	15
16	24	55	8	25	12	6	58	11	17
16	29	10	9	26	13	8	46	13	18
16	33	26	10	27	14	10	38	15	19
16	37	42	11	28	15	12	32	17	20
16	41	59	12	29	16	14	31	19	22
16	46	16	13	♑	18	16	33	20	23
16	50	34	14	1	19	18	40	22	24
16	54	52	15	2	20	20	50	24	25
16	59	10	16	3	21	23	4	26	26
17	3	29	17	4	22	25	21	28	28
17	7	49	18	5	24	27	42	29	29
17	12	9	19	6	25	0 ♓	8	♉	♊
17	16	29	20	7	26	2	37	3	1
17	20	49	21	8	28	5	10	5	3
17	25	9	22	9	29	7	46	6	4
17	29	30	23	10	♒	10	24	8	5
17	33	51	24	11	2	13	7	10	6
17	38	12	25	12	3	15	52	11	7
17	42	34	26	13	4	18	38	13	8
17	46	55	27	14	6	21	27	15	9
17	51	17	28	15	7	24	17	16	10
17	55	38	29	16	9	27	8	18	12
18	0	0	30	17	11	30	0	19	13

Sidereal Time.			10 ♑	11 ♑	12 ♒	Ascen ♈		2 ♉	3 ♊
H.	M.	S.	°	°	°	°	′	°	°
18	0	0	0	17	11	0	0	19	13
18	4	22	1	18	12	2	52	21	14
18	8	43	2	20	14	5	43	23	15
18	13	5	3	21	15	8	33	24	16
18	17	26	4	22	17	11	22	25	17
18	21	48	5	23	19	14	8	27	18
18	26	9	6	24	20	16	53	28	19
18	30	30	7	25	22	19	36	♊	20
18	34	51	8	26	24	22	14	1	21
18	39	11	9	27	25	24	50	2	22
18	43	31	10	29	27	27	23	4	23
18	47	51	11	♒	28	29	52	5	24
18	52	11	12	1	♓	2 ♉	18	6	25
18	56	31	13	2	2	4	39	8	26
19	0	50	14	4	4	6	56	9	27
19	5	8	15	5	6	9	10	10	28
19	9	26	16	6	8	11	20	11	29
19	13	44	17	7	10	13	27	12	♋
19	18	1	18	8	11	15	29	14	1
19	22	18	19	9	13	17	28	15	2
19	26	34	20	11	15	19	22	16	3
19	30	50	21	12	17	21	14	17	4
19	35	5	22	13	19	23	2	18	5
19	39	20	23	15	21	24	47	19	6
19	43	34	24	16	23	26	30	20	7
19	47	47	25	17	25	28	10	21	8
19	52	0	26	18	26	29	46	22	9
19	56	12	27	20	28	1 ♊	19	23	10
20	0	24	28	21	♈	2	50	24	11
20	4	35	29	22	2	4	19	25	12
20	8	45	30	23	4	5	45	26	13

Sidereal Time.			10 ♒	11 ♒	12 ♈	Ascen ♊		2 ♊	3 ♋
H.	M.	S.	°	°	°	°	′	°	°
20	8	45	0	23	4	5	45	26	13
20	12	54	1	25	6	7	9	27	14
20	17	3	2	26	8	8	31	28	14
20	21	11	3	27	9	9	50	29	15
20	25	19	4	29	11	11	7	♋	16
20	29	26	5	♓	13	12	23	1	17
20	33	31	6	1	15	13	37	2	18
20	37	37	7	3	17	14	49	3	19
20	41	41	8	4	19	15	59	4	20
20	45	45	9	5	20	17	8	5	21
20	49	48	10	7	22	18	15	6	22
20	53	51	11	8	24	19	21	7	22
20	57	52	12	10	25	20	25	7	23
21	1	53	13	11	27	21	28	8	24
21	5	53	14	12	29	22	30	9	25
21	9	53	15	13	♉	23	31	10	26
21	13	52	16	14	2	24	31	11	27
21	17	50	17	16	4	25	30	12	28
21	21	47	18	17	5	26	27	12	28
21	25	44	19	18	7	27	24	13	29
21	29	40	20	20	8	28	19	14	♌
21	33	35	21	21	10	29	14	15	1
21	37	29	22	22	11	0 ♋	8	16	2
21	41	23	23	24	12	1	1	17	3
21	45	16	24	25	14	1	54	17	4
21	49	9	25	26	15	2	46	18	4
21	53	1	26	28	17	3	37	19	5
21	56	52	27	29	18	4	27	20	6
22	0	43	28	♈	20	5	17	20	7
22	4	33	29	2	21	6	5	21	8
22	8	23	30	3	22	6	54	22	8

Sidereal Time.			10 ♓	11 ♈	12 ♉	Ascen ♋		2 ♋	3 ♌
H.	M.	S.	°	°	°	°	′	°	°
22	8	23	0	3	22	6	54	22	8
22	12	12	1	4	23	7	42	23	9
22	16	0	2	5	25	8	29	23	10
22	19	48	3	7	26	9	16	24	11
22	23	35	4	8	27	10	3	25	12
22	27	22	5	9	29	10	49	26	13
22	31	8	6	11	♊	11	34	26	13
22	34	54	7	12	1	12	19	27	14
22	38	40	8	13	2	13	3	28	15
22	42	25	9	14	3	13	48	29	16
22	46	9	10	16	4	14	32	29	17
22	49	53	11	17	5	15	15	♌	17
22	53	37	12	18	7	15	58	1	18
22	57	20	13	19	8	16	41	2	19
23	1	3	14	20	9	17	24	2	20
23	4	46	15	22	10	18	6	3	21
23	8	28	16	23	11	18	48	4	21
23	12	10	17	24	12	19	30	4	22
23	15	52	18	25	13	20	11	5	23
23	19	34	19	27	14	20	52	6	24
23	23	15	20	28	15	21	33	6	25
23	26	56	21	29	16	22	14	7	26
23	30	37	22	♉	17	22	54	8	26
23	34	18	23	1	18	23	34	9	27
23	37	58	24	2	19	24	14	9	28
23	41	39	25	4	20	24	54	10	29
23	45	19	26	5	21	25	35	11	♍
23	49	0	27	6	22	26	14	11	0
23	52	40	28	7	22	26	54	12	1
23	56	20	29	8	23	27	33	13	2
24	0	0	30	9	24	28	12	14	3

TABLES OF HOUSES FOR NEW YORK, *Latitude* 40° 43′ N.

Sidereal Time H.	M.	S.	10 ♎ °	11 ♎ °	12 ♏ °	Ascen ♐ °	Ascen ′	2 ♑ °	3 ♒ °
12	0	0	0	29	21	11	7	15	24
12	3	40	1	♏	22	11	52	16	25
12	7	20	2	1	23	12	37	17	26
12	11	0	3	1	24	13	19	17	27
12	14	41	4	2	25	14	7	18	28
12	18	21	5	3	25	14	52	19	29
12	22	2	6	4	26	15	38	20	♓
12	25	42	7	5	27	16	23	21	1
12	29	23	8	6	28	17	11	22	2
12	33	4	9	6	28	17	58	23	3
12	36	45	10	7	29	18	45	24	4
12	40	26	11	8	♐	19	32	25	5
12	44	8	12	9	1	20	20	26	7
12	47	50	13	10	2	21	8	27	8
12	51	32	14	11	2	21	57	28	9
12	55	14	15	12	3	22	43	29	10
12	58	57	16	13	4	23	33	♒	11
13	2	40	17	13	5	24	22	1	12
13	6	23	18	14	6	25	11	2	13
13	10	7	19	15	7	26	1	3	15
13	13	51	20	16	7	26	51	5	16
13	17	35	21	17	8	27	40	6	17
13	21	20	22	18	9	28	32	7	18
13	25	6	23	19	10	29	23	8	19
13	28	52	24	19	10	0 ♑	14	9	20
13	32	38	25	20	11	1	7	10	21
13	36	25	26	21	12	2	0	11	23
13	40	12	27	22	13	2	52	12	24
13	44	0	28	23	13	3	46	13	25
13	47	48	29	24	14	4	41	15	26
13	51	37	30	25	15	5	35	16	27

Sidereal Time H.	M.	S.	10 ♏ °	11 ♏ °	12 ♐ °	Ascen ♑ °	Ascen ′	2 ♒ °	3 ♓ °
13	51	37	0	25	15	5	35	16	27
13	55	27	1	25	16	6	30	17	29
13	59	17	2	26	17	7	27	18	♈
14	3	8	3	27	18	8	23	20	1
14	6	59	4	28	18	9	20	21	2
14	10	51	5	29	19	10	18	22	3
14	14	44	6	♐	20	11	16	23	5
14	18	37	7	1	21	12	15	24	6
14	22	31	8	2	22	13	15	26	7
14	26	25	9	2	23	14	16	27	8
14	30	20	10	3	24	15	17	28	9
14	34	16	11	4	24	16	19	♓	11
14	38	13	12	5	25	17	23	1	12
14	42	10	13	6	26	18	27	2	13
14	46	8	14	7	27	19	32	4	14
14	50	7	15	8	28	20	37	5	16
14	54	7	16	9	29	21	44	6	17
14	58	7	17	10	♑	22	51	8	18
15	2	8	18	10	1	23	59	9	19
15	6	9	19	11	2	25	9	11	20
15	10	12	20	12	3	26	19	12	22
15	14	15	21	13	4	27	31	14	23
15	18	19	22	14	5	28	43	15	24
15	22	23	23	15	6	29	57	16	25
15	26	29	24	16	6	1 ♒	14	18	26
15	30	35	25	17	7	2	28	19	28
15	34	41	26	18	8	3	46	21	29
15	38	49	27	19	9	5	5	22	♉
15	42	57	28	20	10	6	25	24	1
15	47	6	29	21	11	7	46	25	3
15	51	15	30	21	13	9	8	27	4

Sidereal Time H.	M.	S.	10 ♐ °	11 ♐ °	12 ♑ °	Ascen ♒ °	Ascen ′	2 ♓ °	3 ♉ °
15	51	15	0	21	13	9	8	27	4
15	55	25	1	22	14	10	31	28	5
15	59	36	2	23	15	11	56	♈	6
16	3	48	3	24	16	13	23	1	7
16	8	0	4	25	17	14	50	3	9
16	12	13	5	26	18	16	9	4	10
16	16	26	6	27	19	17	50	6	11
16	20	40	7	28	20	19	22	7	12
16	24	55	8	29	21	20	56	9	13
16	29	10	9	♑	22	22	30	11	15
16	33	26	10	1	23	24	7	12	16
16	37	42	11	2	24	25	44	14	17
16	41	59	12	3	26	27	23	15	18
16	46	16	13	4	27	29	4	17	19
16	50	34	14	5	28	0 ♓	45	18	20
16	54	52	15	6	29	2	27	20	22
16	59	10	16	7	♒	4	11	21	23
17	3	29	17	8	2	5	56	23	24
17	7	49	18	9	3	7	43	24	25
17	12	9	19	10	4	9	30	26	26
17	16	29	20	11	5	11	18	27	27
17	20	49	21	12	7	13	8	29	28
17	25	9	22	13	8	14	57	♉	♊
17	29	30	23	14	9	16	48	2	1
17	33	51	24	15	10	18	41	3	2
17	38	12	25	16	12	20	33	5	3
17	42	34	26	17	13	22	25	6	4
17	46	55	27	19	14	24	19	7	5
17	51	17	28	20	16	26	12	9	6
17	55	38	29	21	17	28	7	10	7
18	0	0	30	22	18	30	0	12	9

Sidereal Time H.	M.	S.	10 ♑ °	11 ♑ °	12 ♒ °	Ascen ♈ °	Ascen ′	2 ♉ °	3 ♊ °
18	0	0	0	22	18	0	0	12	9
18	4	22	1	23	20	1	53	13	10
18	8	43	2	24	21	3	48	14	11
18	13	5	3	25	23	5	41	16	12
18	17	26	4	26	24	7	35	17	13
18	21	48	5	27	25	9	27	18	14
18	26	9	6	28	27	11	19	20	15
18	30	30	7	29	28	13	12	21	16
18	34	51	8	♒	♓	15	3	22	17
18	39	11	9	2	1	16	52	23	18
18	43	31	10	3	3	18	42	25	19
18	47	51	11	4	4	20	30	26	20
18	52	11	12	5	5	22	17	27	21
18	56	31	13	6	7	24	4	29	22
19	0	50	14	7	9	25	49	♊	23
19	5	8	15	9	10	27	33	1	24
19	9	26	16	10	12	29	15	2	25
19	13	44	17	11	13	0 ♉	56	3	26
19	18	1	18	12	15	2	37	4	27
19	22	18	19	13	16	4	16	6	28
19	26	34	20	14	18	5	53	7	29
19	30	50	21	16	19	7	30	8	♋
19	35	5	22	17	21	9	4	9	1
19	39	20	23	18	22	10	38	10	2
19	43	34	24	19	24	12	10	11	3
19	47	47	25	20	25	13	41	12	4
19	52	0	26	21	27	15	10	13	5
19	56	12	27	23	29	16	37	14	6
20	0	24	28	24	♈	18	4	15	7
20	4	35	29	25	2	19	29	16	8
20	8	45	30	26	3	20	52	17	9

Sidereal Time H.	M.	S.	10 ♒ °	11 ♒ °	12 ♈ °	Ascen ♉ °	Ascen ′	2 ♊ °	3 ♋ °
20	8	45	0	26	3	20	52	17	9
20	12	54	1	27	5	22	14	18	9
20	17	3	2	29	6	23	35	19	10
20	21	11	3	♓	8	24	55	20	11
20	25	19	4	1	9	26	14	21	12
20	29	26	5	2	11	27	32	22	13
20	33	31	6	3	12	28	46	23	14
20	37	37	7	5	14	0 ♊	3	24	15
20	41	41	8	6	15	1	17	25	16
20	45	45	9	7	16	2	29	26	17
20	49	48	10	8	18	3	41	27	18
20	53	51	11	10	19	4	51	28	19
20	57	52	12	11	21	6	1	29	20
21	1	53	13	12	22	7	9	♋	20
21	5	53	14	13	24	8	16	1	21
21	9	53	15	14	25	9	23	2	22
21	13	52	16	16	26	10	30	3	23
21	17	50	17	17	28	11	33	4	24
21	21	47	18	18	29	12	37	5	25
21	25	44	19	19	♉	13	41	6	26
21	29	40	20	21	2	14	43	6	27
21	33	35	21	22	3	15	44	7	28
21	37	29	22	23	4	16	45	8	28
21	41	23	23	24	6	17	45	9	29
21	45	16	24	25	7	18	44	10	♌
21	49	9	25	27	8	19	42	11	1
21	53	1	26	28	9	20	40	12	2
21	56	52	27	29	11	21	37	12	3
22	0	43	28	♈	12	22	33	13	4
22	4	33	29	1	13	23	30	14	5
22	8	23	30	3	14	24	25	15	5

Sidereal Time H.	M.	S.	10 ♓ °	11 ♈ °	12 ♉ °	Ascen ♊ °	Ascen ′	2 ♋ °	3 ♌ °
22	8	23	0	3	14	24	25	15	5
22	12	12	1	4	15	25	19	16	6
22	16	0	2	5	17	26	14	17	7
22	19	48	3	6	18	27	8	17	8
22	23	35	4	7	19	28	0	18	9
22	27	22	5	8	20	28	53	19	10
22	31	8	6	10	21	29	46	20	11
22	34	54	7	11	22	0 ♋	37	21	11
22	38	40	8	12	23	1	28	21	12
22	42	25	9	13	24	2	20	22	13
22	46	9	10	14	25	3	9	23	14
22	49	53	11	15	27	3	59	24	15
22	53	37	12	17	28	4	49	24	16
22	57	20	13	18	29	5	38	25	17
23	1	3	14	19	♊	6	27	26	17
23	4	46	15	20	1	7	17	27	18
23	8	28	16	21	2	8	3	28	19
23	12	10	17	22	3	8	52	28	20
23	15	52	18	23	4	9	40	29	21
23	19	34	19	24	5	10	28	♌	22
23	23	15	20	26	6	11	15	1	23
23	26	56	21	27	7	12	2	2	23
23	30	37	22	28	8	12	49	2	24
23	34	18	23	29	9	13	37	3	25
23	37	58	24	♉	10	14	22	4	26
23	41	39	25	1	11	15	8	5	27
23	45	19	26	2	12	15	53	5	28
23	49	0	27	3	12	16	41	6	29
23	52	40	28	4	13	17	23	7	29
23	56	20	29	5	14	18	8	8	♍
24	0	0	30	6	15	18	53	9	1

TABLES OF HOUSES FOR GLASGOW, Latitude 55° 58′ N.

Sidereal Time H.	M.	S.	10 ♎ °	11 ♎ °	12 ♏ °	Ascen ♏ °	′	2 ♑ °	3 ♒ °
12	0	0	0	26	15	29	33	3	19
12	3	40	1	27	16	0 ♐	10	4	20
12	7	20	2	28	16	0	46	5	22
12	11	1	3	29	17	1	24	6	23
12	14	41	4	♏	18	2	1	7	24
12	18	21	5	1	18	2	39	7	25
12	22	2	6	2	19	3	16	8	26
12	25	42	7	3	20	3	55	9	27
12	29	23	8	4	20	4	34	10	29
12	33	4	9	4	21	5	13	11	♓
12	36	45	10	5	22	5	54	12	1
12	40	27	11	6	22	6	33	13	3
12	44	8	12	7	23	7	12	14	4
12	47	50	13	7	24	7	52	15	5
12	51	32	14	8	24	8	32	16	6
12	55	14	15	9	25	9	13	17	7
12	58	57	16	9	26	9	53	18	8
13	2	40	17	10	27	10	33	19	10
13	6	24	18	11	27	11	13	20	11
13	10	7	19	12	28	11	53	21	12
13	13	51	20	12	29	12	35	22	13
13	17	36	21	13	29	13	17	23	15
13	21	21	22	14	♐	13	39	25	16
13	25	6	23	15	1	14	42	26	17
13	28	52	24	16	2	15	26	27	19
13	32	38	25	16	2	16	9	28	20
13	36	25	26	17	3	16	52	29	22
13	40	13	27	18	4	17	36	♒	23
13	44	1	28	19	4	18	21	1	24
13	47	49	29	20	5	19	6	3	25
13	51	38	30	20	6	19	51	4	27

Sidereal Time H.	M.	S.	10 ♏ °	11 ♏ °	12 ♐ °	Ascen ♐ °	′	2 ♒ °	3 ♓ °
13	51	38	0	20	6	19	51	4	27
13	55	28	1	21	7	20	37	6	28
13	59	18	2	22	7	21	24	7	♈
14	3	8	3	23	8	22	12	8	1
14	7	0	4	24	9	22	59	10	2
14	10	52	5	25	10	23	46	11	4
14	14	44	6	25	10	24	36	13	5
14	18	37	7	26	11	25	28	14	7
14	22	31	8	27	12	26	17	16	8
14	26	26	9	28	13	27	8	17	9
14	30	21	10	29	14	28	0	19	11
14	34	17	11	30	14	28	53	20	12
14	38	14	12	♐	15	29	45	22	13
14	42	11	13	1	16	0 ♑	39	24	15
14	46	9	14	2	17	1	34	25	16
14	50	9	15	3	18	2	33	27	18
14	54	7	16	4	18	3	31	29	19
14	58	8	17	5	19	4	30	♓	20
15	2	8	18	5	20	5	29	2	22
15	6	10	19	6	21	6	29	4	23
15	10	12	20	7	22	7	32	6	24
15	14	16	21	8	23	8	36	8	26
15	18	19	22	9	24	9	42	10	27
15	22	24	23	10	24	10	50	12	29
15	26	29	24	11	25	12	0	14	♉
15	30	35	25	12	26	13	10	16	1
15	34	42	26	13	27	14	22	18	3
15	38	49	27	13	28	15	37	20	4
15	42	57	28	14	29	16	52	22	6
15	47	6	29	15	♑	18	12	24	7
15	51	16	30	16	1	19	34	26	8

Sidereal Time H.	M.	S.	10 ♐ °	11 ♐ °	12 ♑ °	Ascen ♑ °	′	2 ♓ °	3 ♉ °
15	51	16	0	16	1	19	34	26	8
15	55	26	1	17	2	20	56	28	9
15	59	37	2	18	3	22	21	♈	11
16	3	48	3	19	4	23	51	2	12
16	8	1	4	20	5	25	23	4	13
16	12	13	5	21	6	26	57	6	14
16	16	27	6	22	7	28	35	8	16
16	20	41	7	23	8	0 ♒	16	10	17
16	24	55	8	24	9	2	1	12	18
16	29	11	9	24	10	3	50	14	19
16	33	26	10	25	11	5	43	16	21
16	37	42	11	26	12	7	42	18	22
16	41	59	12	27	14	9	45	20	23
16	46	17	13	28	15	11	52	22	24
16	50	34	14	29	16	14	1	24	26
16	54	52	15	♑	17	16	17	26	27
16	59	11	16	1	18	18	38	28	28
17	3	30	17	2	19	21	6	♉	29
17	7	49	18	3	21	23	39	2	♊
17	12	9	19	4	22	26	15	4	2
17	16	29	20	5	23	28	58	6	3
17	20	49	21	6	24	1 ♓	49	8	4
17	25	10	22	7	26	4	40	9	5
17	29	30	23	8	27	7	36	11	6
17	33	51	24	9	28	10	41	13	7
17	38	13	25	11	♒	13	47	15	9
17	42	34	26	12	1	16	57	16	10
17	46	55	27	13	3	20	12	18	11
17	51	17	28	14	4	23	26	20	12
17	55	38	29	15	5	26	44	21	13
18	0	0	30	16	7	30	0	23	14

Sidereal Time H.	M.	S.	10 ♑ °	11 ♑ °	12 ♒ °	Ascen ♈ °	′	2 ♉ °	3 ♊ °
18	0	0	0	16	7	0	0	23	14
18	4	22	1	17	9	3	17	24	15
18	8	43	2	18	10	6	32	26	16
18	13	5	3	19	12	9	49	27	17
18	17	26	4	20	14	13	4	29	18
18	21	47	5	21	16	16	14	♊	19
18	26	9	6	22	17	19	20	1	21
18	30	30	7	24	19	22	24	3	22
18	34	50	8	25	21	25	20	4	23
18	39	11	9	26	22	28	14	6	24
18	43	31	10	27	24	1 ♉	2	7	25
18	47	51	11	28	26	3	46	8	26
18	52	11	12	♒	28	6	23	9	27
18	56	30	13	1	♓	8	56	11	28
19	0	49	14	2	2	11	22	12	29
19	5	8	15	3	4	13	46	13	♋
19	9	26	16	4	6	15	59	14	1
19	13	43	17	6	8	18	10	15	2
19	18	1	18	7	10	20	16	16	3
19	22	18	19	8	12	22	17	18	4
19	26	34	20	9	14	24	15	19	5
19	30	49	21	11	16	26	8	20	6
19	35	5	22	12	18	27	27	21	7
19	39	19	23	13	20	29	42	22	8
19	43	33	24	14	22	1 ♊	23	23	9
19	47	47	25	15	24	3	1	24	9
19	51	59	26	17	26	4	26	25	10
19	56	12	27	18	28	6	9	26	11
20	0	23	28	20	♈	7	39	27	12
20	4	34	29	21	2	9	4	28	13
20	8	44	30	22	4	10	27	29	14

Sidereal Time H.	M.	S.	10 ♒ °	11 ♒ °	12 ♈ °	Ascen ♊ °	′	2 ♊ °	3 ♋ °
20	8	44	0	22	4	10	27	29	14
20	12	54	1	23	6	11	48	♋	15
20	17	3	2	25	8	13	7	1	16
20	21	11	3	26	10	14	23	2	17
20	25	18	4	27	12	15	57	3	17
20	29	25	5	29	14	16	50	4	18
20	33	31	6	♓	16	18	0	5	19
20	37	36	7	1	18	19	9	6	20
20	41	41	8	3	20	20	17	6	21
20	45	44	9	4	22	21	23	7	22
20	49	48	10	5	24	22	29	8	23
20	53	50	11	7	26	23	32	9	24
20	57	52	12	8	28	24	32	10	25
21	1	52	13	10	♉	25	31	11	25
21	5	53	14	11	1	26	30	12	26
21	9	51	15	12	3	27	28	12	27
21	13	51	16	14	5	28	26	13	28
21	17	40	17	15	6	29	21	14	29
21	21	46	18	17	8	0 ♋	15	15	30
21	25	43	19	18	10	1	8	16	♌
21	29	39	20	20	11	2	1	16	1
21	33	34	21	21	13	2	54	17	2
21	37	29	22	22	14	3	45	18	3
21	41	23	23	23	16	4	35	19	4
21	45	16	24	24	17	5	25	20	5
21	49	8	25	26	19	6	14	20	5
21	53	0	26	28	20	7	3	21	6
21	56	52	27	29	22	7	50	22	7
22	0	42	28	♈	23	8	37	23	8
22	4	32	29	2	24	9	25	23	9
22	8	23	30	3	26	10	11	24	10

Sidereal Time H.	M.	S.	10 ♓ °	11 ♈ °	12 ♉ °	Ascen ♋ °	′	2 ♋ °	3 ♌ °
22	8	23	0	3	26	10	11	24	10
22	12	11	1	4	27	10	56	25	10
22	15	59	2	6	28	11	41	26	11
22	19	47	3	7	29	12	25	26	12
22	23	35	4	8	♊	13	9	27	13
22	27	22	5	10	2	13	53	28	14
22	31	8	6	11	3	14	36	28	14
22	34	54	7	12	4	15	19	29	15
22	38	39	8	14	5	16	0	♌	16
22	42	24	9	15	7	16	42	1	17
22	46	9	10	16	8	17	25	1	18
22	49	53	11	18	9	18	7	2	18
22	53	36	12	19	10	18	47	3	19
22	57	20	13	20	11	19	28	4	20
23	1	3	14	21	12	20	9	4	21
23	4	46	15	23	13	20	49	5	22
23	8	28	16	24	14	21	30	6	22
23	12	10	17	25	15	22	10	6	23
23	15	52	18	26	16	22	48	7	24
23	19	33	19	28	17	23	27	8	25
23	23	15	20	29	18	24	7	8	26
23	26	56	21	♉	19	24	48	9	26
23	30	37	22	1	20	25	27	10	27
23	34	18	23	2	21	26	6	10	28
23	37	58	24	4	22	26	44	11	29
23	41	39	25	5	23	27	22	12	30
23	45	19	26	6	23	28	0	12	♍
23	48	59	27	7	24	28	37	13	1
23	52	40	28	8	25	29	15	14	2
23	56	20	29	10	26	29	51	14	3
24	0	0	30	11	27	0 ♌	29	15	4

INDEX